Wellbeing Champions

Wellbeing Champions is a practical toolkit designed to support primary and secondary schools working with children to co-create a group of Wellbeing Champions. Full of detailed resources to support both the recruitment and training of children and young people to support others in their school settings, this book has been carefully created to ensure that emotions, self-care, resilience, communication and support systems are considered in order to promote and support positive mental health and wellbeing throughout the school setting.

Containing ideas for specific training as well as considering a whole school approach, the resources and tools have been designed to support practitioners, teachers, children and young people to find out what their school does well and to identify areas for development. With a wealth of photocopiable resources, including supervision and training sessions, risk assessments, application forms, feedback forms and certificates, this book offers:

- all the practical resources needed to recruit and interview children and young people for the role, including an outline job description and personal specifications

- a manual that enables teachers to recruit, train and develop the role of Wellbeing Champions within their school

- support to teachers and Wellbeing Champions to develop the role needed within their school

- easy-to-follow, user-friendly sections that can be easily adapted

- lessons and activities that support the Wellbeing Champions and help them understand their role and develop the knowledge and skills to support other young people

Packed full of activities to help promote and support social and emotional skills development and positive mental health and wellbeing within schools at KS2, KS3 and KS4, *Wellbeing Champions* is the ideal resource for teachers and practitioners, focused on pastoral development, mental health and wellbeing and social and emotional development in children and young people.

Alison Waterhouse has worked in mainstream, special education and the independent sector for the past 30 years, specialising in working with children with AEN, including mental health and wellbeing. She has set up and developed an independent therapeutic special school, developed a role as Teacher in Charge of the Social and Emotional Wellbeing of the Whole School Community and has been an inclusion manager and deputy head in mainstream schools. She now works as an independent educational consultant for SEN and wellbeing, is involved in staff training and has her own educational psychotherapy practice. Alison works with children who are referred due to difficulties with self-esteem, anger, anxiety, depression and other mental health needs as well as children with learning differences. Alison is developing the Circles for Learning project in schools, a project that focusses on building positive foundations for mental health and wellbeing. She has undertaken a primary research project and completed an MA in educational research, looking at the impact of the Circles for Learning project in secondary schools.

Wellbeing Champions
A Complete Toolkit for Schools

Alison Waterhouse

Routledge
Taylor & Francis Group

LONDON AND NEW YORK

First published 2021
by Routledge
2 Park Square, Milton Park, Abingdon, Oxon OX14 4RN

and by Routledge
52 Vanderbilt Avenue, New York, NY 10017

Routledge is an imprint of the Taylor & Francis Group, an informa business

© 2021 Alison Waterhouse

The right of Alison Waterhouse to be identified as author of this work has been asserted by her in accordance with sections 77 and 78 of the Copyright, Designs and Patents Act 1988.

All rights reserved. No part of this book may be reprinted or reproduced or utilised in any form or by any electronic, mechanical, or other means, now known or hereafter invented, including photocopying and recording, or in any information storage or retrieval system, without permission in writing from the publishers.

Trademark notice: Product or corporate names may be trademarks or registered trademarks, and are used only for identification and explanation without intent to infringe.

British Library Cataloguing-in-Publication Data
A catalogue record for this book is available from the British Library

Library of Congress Cataloging-in-Publication Data
A catalog record for this book has been requested

ISBN: 978-0-367-43166-2 (hbk)
ISBN: 978-0-367-42986-7 (pbk)
ISBN: 978-1-003-00052-5 (ebk)

Typeset in Avant Garde
by Apex CoVantage, LLC

Contents

	Chapter overview	vii
	Introduction	1
CHAPTER 1	Thinking and finding out	11
CHAPTER 2	Selection and training	99
CHAPTER 3	Supervision: reflective practice	257
CHAPTER 4	Learn, talk and share: developing the role of the Wellbeing Champions	279
	References	287

Chapter overview

INTRODUCTION

Information about the Wellbeing Champions project, including how the resource is set out, what it contains and how to use it.

CHAPTER 1: THINKING AND FINDING OUT

This chapter helps to focus staff on how to collect information as well as understand and identify what school and staff already do well and which areas the WBC could support or develop. It also allows staff to think about some of the potential difficulties that may be encountered and how to both avoid and manage these.

CHAPTER 2: SELECTION AND TRAINING – CREATING SOMETHING SPECIAL TOGETHER

This chapter will include how to recruit WB champions from the whole school community, create a job description with children and young people, set up and develop supervision, write risk assessments and create the Wellbeing Champions Co-ordinators checklist as well as clarify aims and objectives of the project so that a Wellbeing Champions package can be presented to the Senior Leadership Team within the school.

The training part of this chapter will include a range of training sessions for children and young people in both primary and secondary schools.

CHAPTER 3: SUPERVISION

This chapter will include how to set up and run a supervision group, ways of supporting children and young people to refer peers to other support and ways of ensuring the needs of Wellbeing Champions are met.

CHAPTER 4: LEARN, TALK AND SHARE – DEVELOPING THE ROLE OF THE WELLBEING CHAMPIONS

This chapter will include ways of developing the Wellbeing Champions role within each sector of the school community and how to share with other schools.

Introduction

A mentally healthy school is one that adopts a whole-school approach to mental health and wellbeing. It is a school that helps children flourish, learn and succeed by providing opportunities for them, and the adults around them, to develop the strengths and coping skills that underpin resilience. A mentally healthy school sees positive mental health and wellbeing as fundamental to its values, mission and culture. It is a school where child, staff and parent/carer mental health and wellbeing is seen as everybody's business.

Mentally Healthy Schools

In the UK six children and young people (CYP) within every classroom have a diagnosable mental health problem and, sadly, most of them will not seek help for many years. The research is now helping us to understand that the earlier preventative support is available to CYP the more beneficial it is to their positive wellbeing. Unfortunately, many CYP struggle early on to engage with adult-led support. This means that when they do engage their challenges may be more severe and difficult to overcome or find strategies to manage. The Wellbeing Champions Toolkit has been developed to enable staff to help CYP design and set up support for other CYP to access early help, give CYP the skills to support each other and enable these skills to eventually move from the school environment into the surrounding community.

Wellbeing champions are students that champion emotional wellbeing and positive mental health within the school setting and wider community. Champions can initiate, develop and promote positive change and support for the whole school community. Through the work they undertake they are able to challenge beliefs and break down stigmas and barriers to receiving support. Evidence shows that creating a whole school ethos and culture around mental health is key to the wellbeing, attainment and achievement of both students' and staff.

Training children and young people to be wellbeing champions can be beneficial for the school, the children and the young people who attend the school as well as for the children and young people who wish to support others and develop a more positive culture towards mental health and wellbeing.

This training toolkit supports the Mental Health and Wellbeing Lead within a school to recruit, interview and, in collaboration with the CYP, develop the Mental Health and Wellbeing Champions role. This role will be unique to the school environment and may therefore develop differently from that seen in another school.

The training aims to build knowledge of emotions, wellbeing, self-care, resilience, communication and ways of supporting peers. It also helps develop a clear pathway for

Introduction

gaining support from both internal and external professionals. The training will ensure that the Champions have the knowledge, understanding and confidence to promote positive health and wellbeing throughout the school.

It is important to remember that one way of working does not suit all schools. The Wellbeing Champions Toolkit has been designed to support practitioners and CYP to find out what their school does well and what they need and how to develop that provision together. It has been developed around 8 essential elements:

1. Find out and define what you want you want and why.

2. Find the right people to help develop the project.

3. Be creative in building the support that is needed.

4. Relationships are key.

5. Maintain boundaries and keep people safe.

6. Build in reflective group supervision.

7. Be flexible and allow for growth and development.

8. Talk, share and learn more.

Introduction

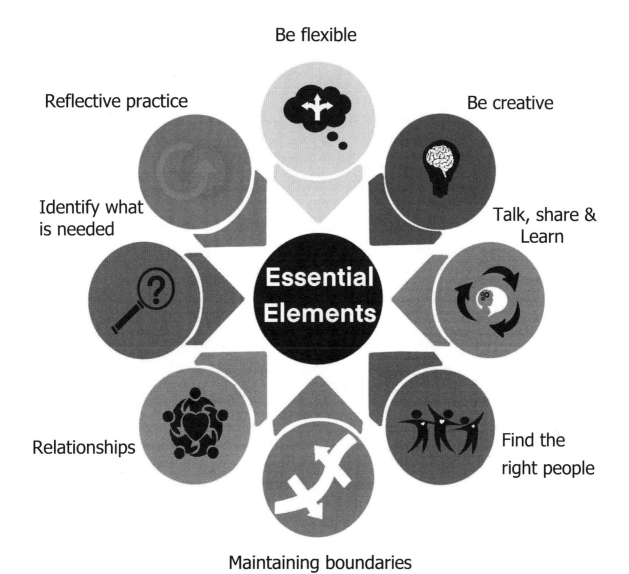

The 8 essential elements to creating a safe, supportive and responsive Wellbeing Champions Team

Introduction

WHAT IS MENTAL HEALTH AND WELLBEING?

I think we are all aware that the mental health and wellbeing of our children and young people is as important as their physical health. Over the past few years it has been recognised that changes need to be implemented in the mental health services for children and young people to both identify and empower them to find the help they need to support, manage and enable them to build and develop resilience.

Mental health and mental ill health are two very different aspects of the same coin. Being and staying mentally healthy and having a diagnosed mental health illness are different things and need distinct supports, approaches and strategies to meet the differing needs they present. Mental health difficulties range from short spells of depression or anxiety to severe, persistent conditions that have the potential to isolate, disrupt and frighten both those who are experiencing them and family and friends who come into contact with them.

Mental health is not just the absence of mental disorder. It is defined as a state of wellbeing in which every individual realises his or her own potential, can cope with the normal stresses of life, can work productively and fruitfully and is able to make a contribution to her or his community. World Health Organisation (2014)

Mental health problems are changes in thought, mood and/or behaviour that impair ability to function (Murphey, Barry, & Vaughn, 2013).

Mental disorders, mental illnesses and psychiatric disorders are conditions that usually cause suffering and impaired functioning and have been diagnosed by a mental health professional.

Like physical health, mental health is something we all have. It can range across a spectrum, from healthy to unwell. It can fluctuate on a daily basis and change over time.

Dodge *et al.* (2012) defined wellbeing as the balance point between an individual's resource pool and the challenges faced. They argued that stable wellbeing is when individuals have the psychological, physical or social skills to manage the challenges encountered. When a person has more challenges than resources their see-saw dips along with their wellbeing and vice versa. The following diagram illustrates this balance and how wellbeing dips if the challenges experienced exceed a person's resources. If, by contrast, the individual has the resources to manage the challenges their wellbeing increases.

Introduction

Problems and difficulties linked to mental health can impact on attainment in school, physical health, relationships, behaviour, exclusions from school and future employment prospects. If, however, mental health can be improved and supported, this can have an impact on a personal, family and community level. Let's take a look at the key statistics:

- One in eight (12.8%) 5- to 19-year-olds had at least one mental disorder when assessed in 2017 (Government Statistical Service, 2017).

- Fifty percent of all mental health problems can be seen by the age of 14, with 75% by the age of 24 (Kessler et al., 2005; Public Health England, 2019).

- Almost 1 in 4 children and young people show some evidence of mental ill health, including anxiety and depression.

- Twenty percent of adolescents may experience a mental health problem in any given year (WHO, 2003).

- Suicide is now the leading cause of death in boys and young men between 5 and 19 years of age.

- One in 12 children and young people self-harm at some point in their lives, though there is evidence that this could be a lot higher.

- Specific mental disorders were grouped into four broad categories: emotional, behavioural, hyperactivity and other less common disorders. Emotional disorders were the most prevalent type of disorder experienced by 5- to 19-year-olds in 2017 (8.1%) (Government Statistical Service, 2017).

- Rates of mental disorders increased with age; 5.5% of 2- to 4-year-old children experienced a mental disorder compared with 16.9% of 17- to 19-year-olds. Caution is needed, however, when comparing rates between age groups due to differences in data collection. For example, teacher reports were available only for 5- to 16-year-olds. Please refer to the Survey Design and Methods Report for full details (Government Statistical Service, 2017).

- Data show an increase over time in the prevalence of mental disorders in 5- to 15-year-olds (the age group covered in all surveys in this series), rising from 9.7% in 1999 and 10.1% in 2004 to 11.2% in 2017 (Government Statistical Service, 2017).

- Emotional disorders have become more common in 5- to 15-year-olds, going from 4.3% in 1999 and 3.9% in 2004 to 5.8% in 2017. All other types of disorders, such as behavioural, hyperactivity and other less common disorders, have remained similar in prevalence for this age group since 1999 (Government Statistical Service, 2017).

Introduction

- Inequality underlies many risk factors for mental health problems in children and young people (Public Health England, 2019).

- There are opportunities to promote good mental health and wellbeing and to build resilience throughout childhood and youth. It's important to take these opportunities both for the health and wellbeing of children and young people and for the health and wellbeing of people throughout their life (Public Health England, 2019).

- Research shows that there is a link between exclusions and emotional health and wellbeing (Ford et al., 2018). Permanent exclusion from school or repeated fixed-term exclusions can have devastating effects on the lives of CYP.

The statistics become rather difficult reading, and for many the topic is so very large that knowing where to being can really be challenging. There is an old adage that says if you want to eat an elephant, you need to do it one bite at a time. I have always found this a helpful way of enabling me to understand that a big project or subject needs to be broken down; then it doesn't seem so big anymore. The process of breaking it down into bite-size pieces is also a very useful one.

The Wellbeing Champions Toolkit is just one way of finding out what is needed within the educational environment you are part of and getting a group of people together who think this is an important area and then doing something about it.

WHAT THE RESEARCH TELLS US

There is a lot of research out there that can guide us in how to work with a group of young people, make changes and create something very special for the environment we are in. We don't have to reinvent the wheel. Toda (2005) describes peer support as "social support by individuals who are similar in age and/or social conditions to the person receiving support."

Cowie and Wallace (2000) highlighted that the difficulties young people face tend to originate from their peer group; therefore, peers may be better able to help solve other pupils' problems. Salmivalli (1999, 2001) showed that adolescents often prefer peer-led anti-bullying interventions; this is often linked to not wanting to accept adult authority telling them what to do.

Within the research exploring peer support, how children and young people are trained has been demonstrated to be of great importance. Following are key features of peer support identified by Cowie and Wallace (2000):

1. CYP are trained to help others outside friendship groups.

2. Training develops key skills (such as communication skills).

3. Training enables CYP to deal with conflict.

Introduction

Similarly, Houlston, Smith, and Jessel (2009) identified communication and interpersonal skills, and Cowie and Smith (2010) highlighted the importance of active listening and problem-solving. The research clearly advocates that peer support is run by pupils for pupils; however, it is also clear in identifying the need for peer supporters to be well supported and supervised by staff. This supervision is a formalised system undertaken by the staff involved. Regular supervision of the peer supporters is essential (e.g. Baginsky, 2004; Cowie & Wallace, 2000). It is recommended that the co-ordinator of the project is fully engaged with the CYP training and that they take the responsibility for meeting scheme objectives, reviewing the project at regular intervals, and being the main point of contact regarding peer support for both staff and pupils (Cowie & Wallace, 2000).

A vital part of any peer mentoring scheme is the school's legal duty to safeguard the welfare of those in its care; therefore, staff members need to ensure that they are aware of any child protection issues disclosed to peer supporters.

Peer support is currently used in many countries around the world. It initially developed in the US in the 1970s and has been widely used in Canada and Australia since the 1980s. In recent years peer support projects have become very popular as a way to lead anti-bullying interventions, in line with the UN Convention on the Rights of the Child (Cowie & Smith, 2010; UN, 1991).

The development of peer support initiatives also seems to be linked to the increasing importance of tackling social issues within schools. Within the UK there are two reported large surveys of peer support use. In their evaluation of the DfES anti-bullying pack Don't Suffer in Silence, Smith and Samara (2003) report peer support systems in place in 50% of primary and secondary schools in the UK. In a later survey by Houlston, Smith and Jessel (2009), it was found that an estimated 61.8% of all English schools use some form of peer support system. Within primary schools befriending was the support most often put in place, followed by mediation, and within secondary schools mentoring was most often used, followed by befriending.

One reason why peer support may be increasingly popular within the UK is possibly due to a high level of government backing. In particular the then Department of Children, Schools and Families (DCSF) contracted a long-term peer mentoring pilot scheme in 180 English schools, run by the Mentoring and Befriending Foundation (MBF) – a national strategic body that focusses on influencing policy and supporting mentoring and befriending at all ages – over 2006 and 2007 (DCSF, 2008). In 2007 DCSF further funded piloting of new types of peer mentoring as part of an initiative to promote peer support in English schools (DCSF, Press notice, 2007/0212).

The findings from the research show that teachers and pupils reported that peer support had a positive impact on school life and that it influenced the quality of the school environment in a number of ways:

1. Where peer support was being undertaken CYP believed that their school was a more caring place. This view was identified as being due to CYP receiving support and experiencing

Introduction

positive outcomes or because they were aware of the support being available to CYP who needed it.

2. The CYP who provided support felt they had contributed to developing a positive school environment.

3. Staff within schools running peer support projects benefited from them, and this then led to a more positive school environment.

4. Behaviours within the schools operating peer support projects became more positive.

5. Social relationships improved.

6. Pupil conflicts and bullying issues were addressed, leading to a safer school environment.

In Naylor and Cowie's (1999) Prince's Trust survey of 51 secondary schools and colleges in the UK, the CYP who used the peer support said they felt it showed that somebody cared about them and how they were feeling. This study included a very large sample of pupils and only schools where peer support had been in place for at least 1 year, suggesting there would have been time for peer support to become embedded and have an impact.

From the recent MBF pilot a representative sample of 24 secondary and 8 primary schools was independently evaluated using student and co-ordinator surveys. The report shows that 62% of mentored at-risk pupils reported that general life satisfaction had increased, and there was a 77% improvement in relatedness – the feeling that others are caring and supportive (MBF, 2011)

Another study – "Peer support and children and young people's mental health: research review" (March 2017) by Nick Coleman, Wendy Sykes and Carola Groom, Independent Social Research (ISR) – found that, according to the small number of robust impact assessments that had been conducted, there is "limited clear and robust evidence of effectiveness of one-to-one school-based projects."

However, the report does add that several studies indicate positive self-reported outcomes for young people who have been supported, in relation to increased happiness or wellbeing, improved self-esteem and confidence and improved social skills or school behaviour. But the research report highlights a number of issues with the concept, including:

1. peer support projects failing or not being sustained due to conflicting priorities in the school, lack of time or an over-reliance on a single co-ordinator

2. low take-up of the scheme by pupils, which can be caused by a lack of trust in peer supporters among the pupil population

Introduction

3. some programmes possibly having a negative impact on young people, with bullying projects potentially exposing children to others with the experience of bullying who may inadvertently reinforce their attitudes and behaviours

4. risk of exposing children to unsettling or overwhelming information about mental illness, particularly in programmes that address more serious mental health issues

The report identified that many of the issues could easily be addressed by ensuring sufficient support to peer supporters. It stated, "Overall, the evidence indicates that different schemes have had varied levels of success, but that peer support programmes can potentially result in a range of positive outcomes for young people."

When we all support each other wondrous things can happen. **Anonymous**

Chapter 1
Thinking and finding out

Thinking and finding out

THE BENEFITS OF PEER SUPPORT

The benefits of the Wellbeing Champions project are wide-ranging. They include supporting children and young people who need support, enabling children and young people to learn skills and strategies that support others and extending the support the school environment offers. The Wellbeing Champions project uses peer-to-peer support. This is based on the evidence that children and young people often find talking to each other easier than talking to an adult, that children and young people can effectively support other children and young people given training and support and that young people often understand the pressures and difficulties their peers are experiencing more easily. There are several key benefits to using peer support within the school environment:

- Collaboration between staff and CYP to create a support network has been shown to develop a particular area. This is mainly due to the incorporation and dialogue that underpin the work. Staff seek out and listen to CYP needs and thoughts and so start to help them create a support network that is heavily influenced by their needs. CYP start to hear and focus on the views and thoughts of the school, so that there is increased understanding of the reason behind policies and practice. This often results in greater understanding across the school environment.

- In working alongside trained staff, children are able to experience a variety of skills and ways of working. This exposure supports their own development of working with others.

- A shared solution approach to working and meeting the needs of others supports a climate of listening, processing and collaboration.

- Peers are often seen to have a greater perceived empathy and respect for the individuals they support.

- There is often great benefit for peer support workers themselves. Research has shown that supporting others is frequently associated with increasing levels of self-esteem, confidence and positive feelings that good is being done.

- Peer support workers often experience an increase in their own ability to cope with mental health problems.

There are many different types of peer support already being used within schools and colleges. Let's discuss some of these now.

Peer listening

A peer supporter who offers a listening service is a person who has been trained in counselling skills that include active listening, verbal and non-verbal communication, confidentiality and problem-solving. Peer supporters who have completed certain training may then go on to offer support to their peers on a formal basis.

Peer education

This involves peers educating peers on specific topics, such as coping with depression, anxiety or addiction. This will generally include a group of peers similar in age, status and background to the people to whom they are delivering material.

Peer learning mentors

Peer tutoring is a model whereby a peer supporter aids a peer, whether of the same age or younger, with his or her academic and social learning. The support offered by the peer tutor can be cross-curricular and take the form of paired reading or writing.

Peer mentoring

One example of this would be a "buddy" system in which people who have received certain training are attached to a new group and act as a friend, mentor and guide to ease people into a new environment.

Another aspect of peer mentoring is that of a positive role model, involving a long-term commitment between the mentor and mentee. The peer mentor is linked to a mentee and has the role of befriender, listener and mediator.

Peer mediation

Conflict resolution is another name for peer mediation. Peer mediators are trained specifically in conflict resolution skills. They help people find solutions to disputes in formal and informal situations.

The Wellbeing Champions Toolkit takes and develops aspects from a range of ways of supporting others to create school-specific wellbeing champions. All the projects described have four clear and shared aspects:

1. CYP support and help other CYP from their own community.

2. Support is planned, thought about and structured.

3. The Peer Support Young People are all trained.

4. The Peer Support Young People are all supervised weekly by the Wellbeing Champions Facilitator.

The Wellbeing Champions Toolkit enables schools to recruit, train and supervise their own wellbeing champions. The Champions themselves then devise and develop the support on offer for others. By doing this the school develops a positive change in culture, ethos and ways of working.

Thinking and finding out

WHAT ARE WELLBEING CHAMPIONS?

Wellbeing champions develop into very different projects within different schools. The Wellbeing Champions Toolkit is a resource that helps practitioners explore and understand the needs of their environment and then select a group of CYP to help them create different ways to meet the needs they have identified.

Wellbeing champions are a group of CYP supported by a member of staff (or group of staff) to meet the needs of the young people within their environment. Some of the ways they may do this are by:

1. Promoting special days or events that focus on wellbeing. This could include Mental Health Days, Anti-Bullying Week, Neurodiverse Awareness week or a range of other special focus days.

2. Supporting the development of positive wellbeing of specific groups within the school community. This may include CYP with parents with MH difficulties, CYP who offend or join gangs, CYP who are in care, CYP with a parent in prison, CYP who are carers at home for siblings or a parent, refugees, CYP who have experienced or are experiencing domestic violence and CYP who are members of the LGBTQ community or have questions about gender identity.

3. Creating a Wellbeing part of the school newsletter that focusses on ways to support wellbeing.

4. Supporting young people who come into the school during transition phases.

5. Creating displays that show the many different aspects of work the school is undertaking to support the wellbeing of CYP, staff and parents.

6. Supporting teachers in delivering special assemblies focussing on wellbeing.

7. Offering a drop-in facility for other CYP.

8. Supporting a buddy scheme in school, focussing on CYP who need a helping hand to manage learning, friendships or transitions.

9. Helping develop the school environment by creating displays, special areas, sensory gardens, healthy eating gardens or calm places within the school.

10. Supporting conflict resolution work or playground monitors.

11. Showing visitors around the school, helping them understand how the school supports the needs of the CYP who attend.

Thinking and finding out

12. Enabling CYP to find a suitable way to have their views and ideas heard and thought about.

13. Signposting CYP who need more specific support.

14. Helping staff share what mental health is and how to support the development of positive mental health and wellbeing.

THE 8 ESSENTIAL ELEMENTS

Making sure your Wellbeing Champions project fits with the 8 essential elements is important and will ensure that your project is safe, focussed, effective and manageable. To support this it is important for you to be clear about what you want the wellbeing champions to do and to identify the objectives of the project.

Wellbeing champions are not a resource that should support CYP with complex mental health needs and are not an alternative to specialist support therapists or counsellors.

Thinking about each of the 8 essential elements is an important starting point for the Wellbeing Champions Facilitator.

Find out what is needed by the children and young people within your school.

Find the right people – both children and adults – to join the team.

Remember that relationships are key to all the work you do.

Thinking and finding out

 Be creative with the solutions you develop.

 Being flexible allows for growth and development.

 Boundaries are really important and keep everyone safe.

 Talk, share and learn more.

 Use weekly reflective group supervision.

THE 8 ESSENTIAL ELEMENTS

FINDING OUT WHAT THE CHILDREN AND SCHOOL NEED AND WHY

The role of the wellbeing champions will change and develop as their work extends or changes. It is aimed to be need-dependent.

When setting up the wellbeing champions it is important to ensure that the 8 essential elements run through all you do.

The first area that has to be explored is understanding what staff, parents and children think are the things the school does well in supporting mental health and wellbeing and what they would like it to do more of to develop further. The voices and views of each group are really important to collect.

Thinking and finding out

Once the views and voices of each group have been collected, an idea of the skills needed by the young people can be understood. This then enables the practitioner leading the WBC to share with the CYP the sort of work that is going to be undertaken and to ask for the young people who are interested to apply for the role.

Gathering information

Gathering information can be an interesting area. It can be done with surveys, questions, discussions or feedback sections on forms. It has to be remembered that it is important to ask all areas of the community what they think. This includes parents, CYP and all staff, including admin staff, cleaners and caretakers. Each group will notice different things, and all views need to be sorted so that a whole picture can be created.

Surveys

Surveys can be a useful way to capture information and thoughts from each group at a particular moment in time. It has to be remembered that surveys are a snapshot of what people are thinking at the time, so they can give an idea of things that may need to be addressed. They can be undertaken electronically or on paper. It is useful to think about the time of year you are going to do this and whether there is a survey the school may already send out, as you may be able to add your questions to this.

Parents

When working with parents it is useful to employ the questionnaires when they are in school and you can approach them personally or as a group. This can be done following a 5-minute presentation about why you are undertaking the questionnaires and what you are hoping to do once you have the results. Parent consultation evenings, transition meetings or school events such as concerts or performances are useful times.

Staff

For staff it is useful to ask for a 15-minute slot at a staff meeting. This enables you to share what you are undertaking and how you are gathering information. You can then hand out the questionnaire and take them back in at the end of the meeting. It is useful if you give the option of people putting their name to the questionnaire or staying anonymous. When working in this way it is also useful to plan how you will get the information from people who are not at the meeting – cleaners, support staff, admin staff, etc. Many of these groups have their own meetings, so it is really worthwhile if you attend these and talk about what you are doing and why.

During these meetings it is often a good idea to ask for people who might be interested in supporting you as you set up the Wellbeing Champions and working with them in a variety of capacities. When thinking about this you can be really creative and set up a wide net of adult supporters. As an example, the caretaker might not be able to work with the CYP; however, they might want to be involved. They could put up notices or check on the condition of posters as

Thinking and finding out

they walk around school in the evening. A member of the admin team might offer to photocopy posters or print off the newsletter or work you want to display on the Wellbeing display board. It is really important to help people think about how they might be involved and the many different skills they bring to the group.

Children and young people

When working with the children it can be useful to explore what they think in a classroom activity, form time or PSHE lesson time. You might want to undertake this so that you can get a feeling for the information and thoughts of the CYP. You could involve a small group of children going around to classrooms, asking for input and explaining how to complete the questionnaire. Each Lead Practitioner will have to choose what works best for both them and their school.

It is really important that the Wellbeing Champions project is reflective of and responsive to the needs of the CYP within the school environment.

FIND THE RIGHT PEOPLE TO HELP DEVELOP THE PROJECT

When starting out on this journey it is really important to think about who needs to be involved and how. This includes both CYP and staff. The Wellbeing Champions project works far better if there is another adult to share the project with. It is really important to remember that the staff who are involved with this project are the role models for the CYP and therefore have to be really good at building and maintaining relationships. They also have to be really strong and effective in communication, emotional literacy and empathy and be very reliable.

If your project is to succeed it is really important to ensure that you have the support and commitment of the Senior Leadership Team. To enable this to happen they need to be involved with the development of the project from the beginning and kept up to date with the data you collect as well as your plans and key objectives.

BE CREATIVE IN BUILDING THE SUPPORT THAT IS NEEDED

Once a range of information has been collected that shows what the school does well, and also helps you understand the areas where it could do better, it is important to try and identify areas that could be developed and supported by the Wellbeing Champions Team. A real focus of the work is giving the CYP who volunteer for the project the time and space to co-create with you ways of tackling the issues you have identified. The specific strategies need to be developed by the team itself and will form part of the training with the CYP. It is during the training that you will be able to help them explore, be curious and take a creative solution-focussed approach to solving the issues.

Thinking and finding out

An example of this may be that the information collected shows that CYP are finding playtime difficult to manage. This may be a result of several factors, including friendships, self-regulation and conflict. Each area will need to be addressed and specific ways of supporting and developing skills identified.

RELATIONSHIPS ARE KEY

Ensuring that CYP have the experience of safe and trusted relationships, both as part of the Wellbeing Champions Team and for the CYP they support, is vital if the project is to be successful. When identifying and selecting your Champions it is therefore really important to focus on these skills both individually and as a group. This thread will also run through all the training you put in place and will be a strong element of the ongoing supervision of the Champions.

A safe, stable and nurturing relationship with you as their facilitator will ensure that the CYP are able to manage their own emotions and self-regulate, be able to recognise and respond appropriately to the emotional states of others and develop close and supportive relationships with the CYP they support.

Considerable time and energy will need to be directed to enabling the Wellbeing Champions to initiate, develop and manage the relationships with the CYP they support.

It will be just as important for you as their facilitator and any staff involved in the project to develop secure and positive relationships with each of the Wellbeing Champions. This will enable exciting and positive training sessions as well as positive and effective supervision.

A focus on relationships enables you to ensure that the Wellbeing Champions project is developed by the CYP for the CYP of their community. It is not a project that can just be dropped into a school, as it is designed to be tailor-made by the Wellbeing Champions and their facilitator to meet the specific needs of their community. The project will be a collaboration between the adults and the CYP that will then be co-created and co-delivered.

MAINTAIN BOUNDARIES AND KEEP PEOPLE SAFE

It is really important that your Wellbeing Champions project is safe, has a good process for communication and is clear about confidentiality. All of these areas are addressed through the training and the weekly supervision sessions.

The Wellbeing Champions project is designed to be a preventative and early intervention way of working and not a specialist programme. For CYP who need specific support for mental health, other organisations and professions will need to be accessed.

As the Wellbeing Champions Facilitator you do not need to be an expert in mental health. You do, however, need to be a person who understands the importance of relationships, has a good level of emotional literacy and wants to work with CYP to develop a provision within your school that supports other CYP.

The Wellbeing Champions will explore why confidentiality is of great importance and also how to address any safeguarding or urgent/severe mental health issues. It is very important that the training allows CYP to feel able to manage the situations and interactions they will be asked to deal with and that they are clear about what they can do and who they can refer on to. During the training a range of role play scenarios are used to support their knowledge and understanding. It will also be very important that they hear the limitations of their role during the training and are helped to understand why this is important. It is also important to help them understand how they fit into the provision the school already has in place.

Ongoing supervision ensures that CYP do not feel abandoned, left to flounder or overwhelmed by the work and support they are providing. During supervision it is really important for the Wellbeing Champions to be helped to understand what they can share and what needs to be shared with specific individuals outside of the supervision group. By ensuring that all understand this process both the Wellbeing Champions and the CYP they are supporting will feel safe.

Part of the training will explore what is suitable for the Wellbeing Champions to work with and when it is right to find support or to signpost to another support within or outside of school. It is vital that they see themselves as one support mechanism in a web of many.

BE FLEXIBLE AND ALLOW FOR GROWTH AND DEVELOPMENT

Being flexible is a key aspect of both the setting up of the Wellbeing Champions and the work they will undertake. When collecting the information about what the school does well and what staff, parents and children would like it to do better it will be important to think about ways in which this can be achieved with the time, resources and capacity you have. There are some great ways of working already being developed, some of which will suit your environment well and some of which will need to be adapted.

During the training the Wellbeing Champions will work on problem-solving and solution-focussed ways of working, respect and self-determination. Part of the training will be focussed on developing the skills of active listening as a way of helping CYP feel understood and then engaging in working with the Champions on what or how to solve the issues and difficulties they face. This will include a range of options, some of which will mean talking or working with other professionals.

Thinking and finding out

As the Wellbeing Champions work you will become more aware of the needs that are being presented and of systems and procedures that could be changed to support these in a better way. You may also find that other needs become more apparent just by having the Wellbeing Champions accessible within the school environment.

TALK, SHARE AND LEARN MORE

As your work with the Wellbeing Champions grows and develops you will need to share with CYP as well as staff and parents. You may even be able to share with other schools or be asked to support the development of Wellbeing Champions in other schools. I would strongly urge you to take up this opportunity. When sharing work with others you develop your own practice and knowledge as well as start a journey for other people. Imagine what it would have been like if you could have had someone help you with your project at the beginning.

Not only will you be asked to share or talk about the work of the Wellbeing Champions, but the Champions themselves will also be asked to share their experience. This is a really positive experience for them and one that can be really exciting.

As with any new project it is really valuable to keep a record of how the project develops – the ups as well as the downs. It may seem a tedious added burden, but with the help of your Champions it is one very much worth undertaking. To share these memories and experiences as you develop the role can be really beneficial for all.

REFLECTIVE GROUP SUPERVISION

Reflective group supervision ensures that you as the WBC Facilitator are aware of the WBC and how they are managing the role, that any issues are spotted and dealt with quickly and professionally, that essential information is passed on to other adults within the school and that the wellbeing of all concerned is supported so that the team can thrive and make a difference. This is an essential element of the Wellbeing Champions' ability to undertake their role both safely and in a professional way.

MENTAL HEALTH AND WELLBEING WHOLE SCHOOL APPROACH

It is a useful idea to map all the things your school is already doing to support MHWB so that you are very clear of the areas the school is working on and how the work of the WBC will complement and fit in with this. This also enables you to clearly see which staff are already leading in specific areas and who you could approach for support or guidance when setting up the WBC.

When undertaking an audit there are many different tools freely available on the internet. All tend to look at 8 different areas and then have a range of questions linked to each one.

Thinking and finding out

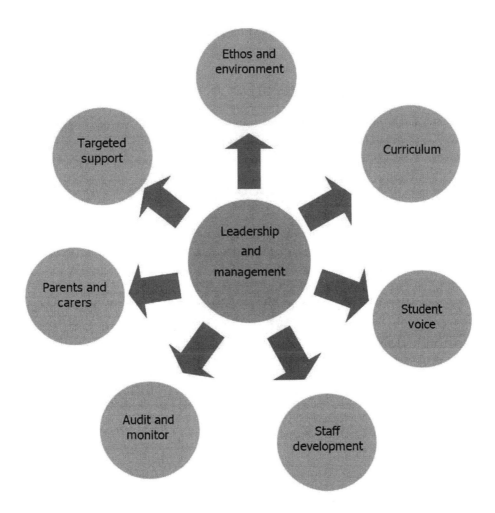

Another important area to consider is how you will manage the ongoing work as Supervisor for the WBC. Will this be something you do on your own or will you be working with one or two other members of staff? It is really useful to involve other members of staff if at all possible, as this ensures that the work of the WBC is not compromised if you're sick or have to focus your time on other things at certain points. It is also useful, in that it means that the work becomes more sustainable if staff move or take up other roles within the school.

A huge part of the work is focussed at the beginning of the project on identifying the roles and responsibilities of the WBC and recruiting and training them. All of these roles can be carried out by different people, if needed, or by one person. Once the champions are up and running the majority of the work is focussed on ongoing training and weekly supervision. It is really helpful to plan how this work will be undertaken. If you are a part of a large school you may put a small team of people around the WBC. This might involve TAs or Behaviour Support Assistants, ELSAs or Learning Mentors, with a Teacher or Wellbeing Lead overseeing the work. If, however, you are from a small primary school, you may be undertaking this new adventure on your own. It is useful to think and plan how these different roles will be undertaken and the time commitment of each.

One of the most important areas is that of ongoing weekly supervision for the WBC. This will need to involve all the WBC and will be discussed in more detail later in the chapter.

Thinking and finding out

Table of questions to help think about the information already gathered.

What things does your school already have in place?
What are the 3 key strengths identified by staff, children and parents?
What are the 3 key areas identified by staff, children and parents that need to grow?
Who are the people who have expressed an interest?

HOW DOES THE WBC ROLE FIT WITHIN THE SCHOOL?

Once the information is collected from staff, CYP and parents it is useful to put this into a table.

THINGS WE DO WELL	THINGS WE ARE WORKING ON	THINGS WE WANT TO DO BETTER	WAYS IN WHICH OUR WBC CAN SUPPORT THIS AREA
• Good PSHE curriculum that focusses on MHWB and areas that can support the development of positive MHWB	• Developing special days	• Knowing what days are coming up each term	• Support assemblies • Go and talk to different classrooms about the focus day • Ensure that the Wellbeing boards have information on them about the focus days

Now that you have collected a range of information about how MHWB is being both developed and promoted in school and have completed your table you are aware of how the WBC can support the different areas within the school environment and the skills you might need to have or build into the training.

WHICH CHILDREN?

Now it is time to think about how many WBC you need and which year groups you will open this up to.

In primary schools I suggest this is for children in years 4–6. This will give you a good range of children across the school and will allow for the work to continue when the Y6 children move on as well as give you time to train the next group.

In secondary school it is often good to open this work to children in years 8–10. Those in year 7 have lots to focus on, like settling into school, making new friends and getting to grips with timetables, different teachers and a whole new way of working.

Thinking and finding out

The next question is how many CYP to train. I would strongly suggest that you train a few more than you think you need. You will always get CYP who drop out for one reason or another. The number really depends on what you would like your WBC to do and how you would like them to work. If you want to ensure that you have a drop-in facility, then you need to make sure you have enough WBC to run this each day. Most CYP will give up only one lunchtime to do this. If you want your WBC to work in other areas as well – for instance on the playground – then you need to make sure you have sufficient time to manage both activities on a daily basis. This often means that you personally train all your champions.

A good number to train is between 12 and 20. This enables you to have enough CYP to have group activities and discussions but also makes the number small enough to really enable people to get to know each other and form a positive group ethos. There is nothing more disheartening for children and young people than to be chosen to do something and then have nothing to actually do.

Once you have worked out roughly how your WBC can support the work of your school and also meet the needs of the CYP and you have decided how many you think you need, it is time to recruit them.

The next question to ask yourself is how and when you will train your WBC. The training is laid out in Chapter 3. The sessions and activities are interchangeable and allow you to choose and modify them depending on your group and what you would like to support them with as well as what aspects of the role you are training them for. When and where to train them will really depend on your own timetable, who else will be supporting you and when you feel you would be able to access the CYP. Within primary school this is often less tricky than within secondary school. In secondary school you might have the option of form time or lunchtime or use different times and days so that they don't miss the same lessons. Another successful time is after school, when you know the CYP will not be missing lessons, or during enrichment times. Likewise, if your school focusses on a wellbeing week, then you could use time within this.

THINKING ABOUT POTENTIAL DIFFICULTIES

When thinking about setting up a Wellbeing Champions Group many staff have concerns about the safety of and risk to both the Champions and the CYP they support. It is therefore really important to collect these concerns and ensure that they are carefully answered and addressed. The concerns that are often raised are:

1. Failure to address the MH needs that have been raised in a session with the Wellbeing Champions

2. Safeguarding issues not being properly understood or reported.

Thinking and finding out

3. Breaking confidentiality

4. Too much stress put on the CYP who are acting as Champions, which then has a negative impact on wellbeing

5. CYP not using the Champions, as they are too concerned about other CYP finding out and making fun of them

6. Wellbeing Champions giving the wrong advice and causing harm to another CYP

RISK ASSESSMENT AND SAFEGUARDING

As with all activities with CYP it is very important to complete a risk assessment and ensure that the safety of the Wellbeing Champions is safeguarded as well as the safety of other CYP who may approach them for help. As long as you ensure that you follow the school's well-thought-out procedures and policies, both needs will be met.

When you have completed your risk assessment make sure that you discuss it with a senior leader within the school. If your school has a Wellbeing Lead, they would be the first port of call.

Make sure you have re-read the school's safeguarding policy and understood how the work you and your WBC will be supported by this. If the policy raises any questions, then meet with your Wellbeing Lead or a member of your SLT and discuss any questions or issues you may have.

It is advisable to write a WBC document that clearly shows the process you intend to follow, the training you will be putting in place, risk assessments for the work and procedures the WBC will follow. Another important aspect is showing how you will use weekly supervision to ensure that your WBC are supported and any issues or difficulties are quickly picked up and dealt with.

Let's inspire each other to create amazing things.

Thinking and finding out

RESOURCES

Staff Questionnaire
Staff Questionnaire Results Sheet
Parents' Questionnaire
Parents' Questionnaire Results Sheet
Young People's Questionnaire
Young People's Questionnaire Results Sheet
Children's Questionnaire
Children's Questionnaire Results Sheet
Mental Health and Wellbeing Whole School Audit
Mental Health and Wellbeing Table of Results Blank
Recruitment Poster for Wellbeing Champions Primary
Recruitment Poster for Wellbeing Champions Secondary
Introducing the Wellbeing Champions to Staff Session Primary and Secondary
Introducing the Wellbeing Champions to Parents' Session Primary
Introducing the Wellbeing Champions to Parents' Session Secondary
Introducing the Wellbeing Champions Assembly Session
Risk Assessment Example Primary
Risk Assessment Example Secondary
Risk Assessment Blank
Wellbeing Champions Individual Areas Action Plan Example Primary
Wellbeing Champions Individual Areas Action Plan Example Secondary
Wellbeing Champions Individual Areas Action Plan Blank
Wellbeing Champions Complete Action Plan Blank
Proposal Document Checklist Cover Sheet for Senior Leadership Team
Flow Diagram for Setting Up the WBC
How to Become a WBC Flow Chart for Children and Young People
Mental Health and Wellbeing Support Pyramid
Wellbeing Champions Application Form
Wellbeing Champions Reference Form
Flow Chart to Show How Children and Young People Can Be Referred

Thinking and finding out

STAFF QUESTIONNAIRE

As a Senior Leadership Team we believe it is of real importance to support the mental health and wellbeing of staff, children and parents. We are very aware that we do some things well and that there are other areas we are working on and trying to develop.

We are undertaking an audit of the work we already have in place so that we can develop the provision and way we work over the year ahead. To ensure that we collect information from across our community we are asking you as members of our staff team to complete this short questionnaire.

Using a scale of Red, Amber and Green, please provide your rating of the school's performance for each of the statements. Please try to respond as honestly as possible and describe the evidence you have for giving this rating. Where possible, please suggest any ideas you might have for improving the provision.

Red Disagree   Amber Neither disagree nor agree   Green Agree

STATEMENT	CHOOSE YOUR RATING . . .	I KNOW THIS BECAUSE . . .	THIS COULD BE EVEN BETTER IF . . .
I believe that emotional wellbeing and mental health are important areas for the school to address.	Red Amber Green		
I believe that our school has an important role to play in the positive emotional wellbeing and mental health of my child.	Red Amber Green		
I understand the importance of emotional wellbeing and mental health and how they can affect children's ability to learn and manage in school.	Red Amber Green		
I understand how I as a teacher can contribute to the emotional wellbeing and mental health of children within the school environment.	Red Amber Green		

Thinking and finding out

I believe that everyone involved with our school needs to support and look out for each other when it comes to emotional wellbeing and mental health. This includes staff, parents and children and young people.	Red	Amber	Green
I believe our school really cares about the emotional wellbeing and mental health of everyone involved with the school. This includes all the people who work within the school, the children and the parents and carers.	Red	Amber	Green
I think the school values emotional wellbeing and mental health and understands their importance to children's learning.	Red	Amber	Green
I think the school values emotional wellbeing and mental health and understands their importance to behaviour.	Red	Amber	Green
Our school actively encourages all staff to be open about how they are feeling.	Red	Amber	Green
I would feel comfortable talking about my own emotional wellbeing and mental health with people in school if I needed to.	Red	Amber	Green
I believe that increasing the knowledge and understanding of staff in the areas of mental health and wellbeing is a priority for the school.	Red	Amber	Green

Copyright material from Alison Waterhouse (2021), *Wellbeing Champions*, Routledge

Thinking and finding out

I believe that I have the knowledge and skills needed to address the emotional wellbeing and mental health of the children and young people I teach/work with.	**Red**	**Amber**	**Green**
I feel able to identify signs of emotional or mental distress in both pupils and colleagues.	**Red**	**Amber**	**Green**
I feel comfortable in knowing what to do next if I see someone with signs of emotional or mental distress.	**Red**	**Amber**	**Green**
I believe the school offers good quality support for children and young people with emotional wellbeing and mental health difficulties.	**Red**	**Amber**	**Green**
Name:	I wish to be anonymous		Date

Thinking and finding out

STAFF QUESTIONNAIRE RESULTS

Red Disagree   Amber Neither disagree nor agree   Green Agree

STATEMENT	RED	AMBER	GREEN
I believe that emotional wellbeing and mental health are important areas for the school to address.			
I believe that our school has an important role to play in the positive emotional wellbeing and mental health of my child.			
I understand the importance of emotional wellbeing and mental health and how they can affect children's ability to learn and manage in school.			
I understand how I as a teacher can contribute to the emotional wellbeing and mental health of children within the school environment.			
I believe that everyone involved with our school needs to support and look out for each other when it comes to emotional wellbeing and mental health. This includes staff, parents and children and young people.			
I believe our school really cares about the emotional wellbeing and mental health of everyone involved with the school. This includes all the people who work within the school, the children and the parents and carers.			
I think the school values emotional wellbeing and mental health and understands their importance to children's learning.			
I think the school values emotional wellbeing and mental health and understands their importance to behaviour.			
Our school actively encourages all staff to be open about how they are feeling.			

Copyright material from Alison Waterhouse (2021), *Wellbeing Champions*, Routledge

Thinking and finding out

I would feel comfortable talking about my own emotional wellbeing and mental health with people in school if I needed to.				
I believe that increasing the knowledge and understanding of staff in the areas of mental health and wellbeing is a priority for the school.				
I believe that I have the knowledge and skills needed to address the emotional wellbeing and mental health of the children and young people I teach/work with.				
I feel able to identify signs of emotional or mental distress in both pupils and colleagues.				
I feel comfortable in knowing what to do next if I see someone with signs of emotional or mental distress.				
I believe the school offers good quality support for children and young people with emotional wellbeing and mental health difficulties.				
Total number of forms returned				
Date				

PARENTS' QUESTIONNAIRE

Thinking and finding out

All staff within our school are very very aware of the importance of supporting children's mental health and wellbeing. We are very aware that we do some things well and that there are other areas we are working on and trying to develop.

We are undertaking an audit of the work we already have in place so that we can develop the provision and way we work over the year ahead. To ensure that we collect information from across our community we are asking you as parents and carers to complete this short questionnaire.

Using a scale of Red, Amber and Green, please provide your rating of the school's performance for each of the statements. Please try and respond as honestly as possible and describe the evidence you have for giving this rating. Where possible, please suggest any ideas you might have for improving the provision.

Red Disagree   **Amber** Neither disagree nor agree   **Green** Agree

STATEMENT	CHOOSE YOUR RATING . . .	I KNOW THIS BECAUSE . . .	THIS COULD BE EVEN BETTER IF . . .
I believe that emotional wellbeing and mental health are important areas for the school to address.	Red Amber Green		
I believe that our school has an important role to play in the positive emotional wellbeing and mental health of my child.	Red Amber Green		
I understand the importance of emotional wellbeing and mental health and how they can affect my child's ability to learn and manage in school.	Red Amber Green		
I understand how I as a parent can contribute to the emotional wellbeing and mental health of my child within the school environment.	Red Amber Green		
I believe that everyone involved with our school needs to support and look out for each other when it comes to emotional wellbeing and mental health. This includes staff, parents and children and young people.	Red Amber Green		

Copyright material from Alison Waterhouse (2021), *Wellbeing Champions*, Routledge

Thinking and finding out

I believe our school really cares about the emotional wellbeing and mental health of everyone involved with the school. This includes all the people who work within the school, the children and the parents and carers.	**Red Amber Green**	
I think the school values emotional wellbeing and mental health and understands their importance to learning.	**Red Amber Green**	
I think the school values emotional wellbeing and mental health and understands their importance to behaviour.	**Red Amber Green**	
Our school actively encourages parents to be open about how they and their children are feeling.	**Red Amber Green**	
I would feel comfortable talking about my own emotional wellbeing and mental health with people in school if I needed to.	**Red Amber Green**	
I would feel comfortable talking about my child's emotional wellbeing and mental health with staff in school if I needed to.	**Red Amber Green**	
The school asks for my thoughts, opinions, views and needs about its approach to emotional wellbeing and mental health, and it listens to my voice.	**Red Amber Green**	
Name:	I wish to be anonymous	Date

Thinking and finding out

PARENTS' QUESTIONNAIRE RESULTS

Red Disagree   Amber Neither disagree nor agree   Green Agree

STATEMENT	RED	AMBER	GREEN
I believe that emotional wellbeing and mental health are important areas for the school to address.			
I believe that our school has an important role to play in the positive emotional wellbeing and mental health of my child.			
I understand the importance of emotional wellbeing and mental health and how they can affect my child's ability to learn and manage in school.			
I understand how I as a parent can contribute to the emotional wellbeing and mental health of my child within the school environment.			
I believe that everyone involved with our school needs to support and look out for each other when it comes to emotional wellbeing and mental health. This includes staff, parents and children and young people.			
I believe our school really cares about the emotional wellbeing and mental health of everyone involved with the school. This includes all the people who work within the school, the children and the parents and carers.			
I think the school values emotional wellbeing and mental health and understands their importance to learning.			

Copyright material from Alison Waterhouse (2021), *Wellbeing Champions*, Routledge

Thinking and finding out

I think the school values emotional wellbeing and mental health and understands their importance to behaviour.	Our school actively encourages parents to be open about how they and their children are feeling.	I would feel comfortable talking about my own emotional wellbeing and mental health with people in school if I needed to.	I would feel comfortable talking about my child's emotional wellbeing and mental health with staff in school if I needed to.	The school asks for my thoughts, opinions, views and needs about its approach to emotional wellbeing and mental health, and it listens to my voice.	Total number of forms returned	Date

YOUNG PEOPLE'S QUESTIONNAIRE

As a school we believe it is really important to support staff, children and parents with their mental health and wellbeing.

We know that there are some things we do really well. We also know that there are some areas in which we could do better.

We are collecting information on what you think so that we can get better in the way we work during the year. It is really important for us to hear what you think and why, so we would like it if you would fill out this questionnaire.

Using a scale of Red, Amber and Green, please tell us what you think about how we are doing. Please try and respond as honestly as possible and tell us what makes you think this. If you have any ideas you think would make what we do better, please tell us.

Red Disagree   Amber Neither disagree nor agree   Green Agree

STATEMENT	CHOOSE YOUR RATING . . .			I KNOW THIS BECAUSE . . .	THIS COULD BE EVEN BETTER IF . . .
In our school, we learn about how important it is to talk about our feelings and emotions.	Red	Amber	Green		
My teachers help my class talk about how we are feeling.	Red	Amber	Green		
I think my school really cares about me and how I am feeling.	Red	Amber	Green		
I can tell when someone is feeling sad, angry, happy or worried.	Red	Amber	Green		
I believe I can make a difference if someone else is feeling worried or unhappy.	Red	Amber	Green		

Thinking and finding out

I think my school really cares about all the children who come here and how they are feeling.	Red	Amber	Green	
I would be able to talk to a member of staff in school about how I was feeling if needed to.	Red	Amber	Green	
If I get upset one of the teachers always notices and tries to help me.	Red	Amber	Green	
If something happens on the playground I feel able to talk to the staff on duty about it.	Red	Amber	Green	
The staff on duty at playtime and lunchtime help me sort things out if I need them to.	Red	Amber	Green	
I think my teachers know when I am feeling worried or unhappy.	Red	Amber	Green	
I can get help in my school when I am feeling worried or unhappy.	Red	Amber	Green	
I think my school really cares about what I think and asks and listens to what I have to say.	Red	Amber	Green	
Name:		I wish to be anonymous		Date

Copyright material from Alison Waterhouse (2021), *Wellbeing Champions*, Routledge

YOUNG PEOPLE'S QUESTIONNAIRE RESULTS

As a school we believe it is really important to support staff, children and parents with their mental health and wellbeing.

We know that we do some things really well. We also know that there are some areas in which we could do better.

We are collecting information on what you think so that we can get better in the way we work during the year. It is really important for us to hear what you think and why, so we would like it if you would fill out this questionnaire.

Using a scale of Red, Amber and Green, please tell us what you think about how we are doing. Please try and respond as honestly as possible and tell us what makes you think this. If you have any ideas you think would make what we do better, please tell us.

Red Disagree   Amber Neither disagree nor agree   Green Agree

STATEMENT	RED	AMBER	GREEN
In our school, we learn about how important it is to talk about our feelings and emotions.			
My teachers help my class talk about how we are feeling.			
I think my school really cares about me and how I am feeling.			
I can tell when someone is feeling sad, angry, happy or worried.			
I believe I can make a difference if someone else is feeling worried or unhappy.			
I think my school really cares about all the children who come here and how they are feeling.			

Thinking and finding out

I would be able to talk to a member of staff in school about how I was feeling if needed to.							
If I get upset one of the teachers always notices and tries to help me.							
If something happens on the playground I feel able to talk to the staff on duty about it.							
The staff on duty at playtime and lunchtime help me sort things out if I need them to.							
I think my teachers know when I am feeling worried or unhappy.							
I can get help in my school when I am feeling worried or unhappy.							
I think my school really cares about what I think and asks and listens to what I have to say.							
Total number of forms returned							
Date							

Thinking and finding out

CHILDREN'S QUESTIONNAIRE

As a school we believe it is really important to support staff, children and parents with their mental health and wellbeing.

We know that we do some things really well. We also know that there are some areas in which we could do better.

We are collecting information on what you think so that we can get better in the way we work during the year. It is really important for us to hear what you think and why, so we would like it if you would fill out this questionnaire.

Using a scale of Red, Amber and Green, please tell us what you think about how we are doing. Please try and respond as honestly as possible and tell us what makes you think this. If you have any ideas you think would make what we do better, please tell us.

Red Disagree   Amber Neither disagree nor agree   Green Agree

STATEMENT	CHOOSE YOUR RATING			I KNOW THIS BECAUSE . . .	THIS COULD BE EVEN BETTER IF . . .
In our school, we learn about how important it is to talk about our feelings and emotions.	Red	Amber	Green		
My teacher helps my class talk about how we are feeling.	Red	Amber	Green		
I think my school really cares about me and how I am feeling.	Red	Amber	Green		
I can tell when someone is feeling sad, angry, happy or worried.	Red	Amber	Green		
I believe I can make a difference if someone else is feeling worried or unhappy.	Red	Amber	Green		

Copyright material from Alison Waterhouse (2021), *Wellbeing Champions*, Routledge

Thinking and finding out

I think my school really cares about all the children who come here and how they are feeling.	Red	Amber	Green	
I would be able to talk to a member of staff in school about how I was feeling if needed to.	Red	Amber	Green	
If I get upset one of the teachers always notices and tries to help me.	Red	Amber	Green	
If something happened at playtime I would be able to talk to the staff on duty.	Red	Amber	Green	
If I get upset at playtime people notice and try and help me.	Red	Amber	Green	
I think my teachers know when I am feeling worried or unhappy.	Red	Amber	Green	
I can get help in my school when I am feeling worried or unhappy.	Red	Amber	Green	
I think my school really cares about what I think and asks and listens to what I have to say.	Red	Amber	Green	
Name:		I wish to be anonymous		Date

CHILDREN'S QUESTIONNAIRE RESULTS

Red Disagree   Amber Neither disagree nor agree   Green Agree

STATEMENT	RED	AMBER	GREEN
In our school, we learn about how important it is to talk about our feelings and emotions.			
My teacher helps my class talk about how we are feeling.			
I think my school really cares about me and how I am feeling.			
I can tell when someone is feeling sad, angry, happy or worried.			
I believe I can make a difference if someone else is feeling worried or unhappy.			
I think my school really cares about all the children who come here and how they are feeling.			
I would be able to talk to a member of staff in school about how I was feeling if needed to.			
If I get upset one of the teachers always notices and tries to help me.			
If something happened at playtime I would be able to talk to the staff on duty.			
If I get upset at playtime people notice and try and help me.			
I think my teachers know when I am feeling worried or unhappy.			
I can get help in my school when I am feeling worried or unhappy.			
I think my school really cares about what I think and asks and listens to what I have to say.			
Total number of forms returned			
Date			

Thinking and finding out

Thinking and finding out

Mental health and wellbeing audit

Name of school:

Completed by:

Date:

Shared with SLT:

Shared with governors:

Thinking and finding out

Why is supporting mental health and wellbeing important?

It is now understood that a child's emotional health and wellbeing influence not only their cognitive ability and development but also their physical and social health and mental wellbeing into adulthood. Children and young people's mental health and wellbeing include:

- the ability to develop psychologically, emotionally, creatively, intellectually and spiritually
- the capacity to initiate, develop and sustain mutually satisfying personal relationships
- the ability to become aware of others and empathise with them
- the ability to play and learn
- the ability to develop a moral sense of what is right and wrong
- the ability to be able to face and resolve problems and setbacks and learn from them
- the ability to both use and enjoy solitude

DfE, 2016

Poor mental health in childhood has an impact on future health and social and personal outcomes. It is estimated that one in ten 5- to 16-year-olds have a diagnosed mental health disorder and that almost 1 in 4 show some evidence of mental ill health, including anxiety and depression. Half of all mental health problems in adults manifest by the age of 14 and 75% by the age of 24. Suicide is the most common cause of death for young boys aged 5–19 years and the second most common for girls of the same age.

Copyright material from Alison Waterhouse (2021), *Wellbeing Champions*, Routledge

Thinking and finding out

Guidance for completing the audit

In 2015 Public Health England and the Children's and Young People's Mental Health Coalition identified 8 key principles for emotional health and wellbeing. At the heart of these are leadership and management.

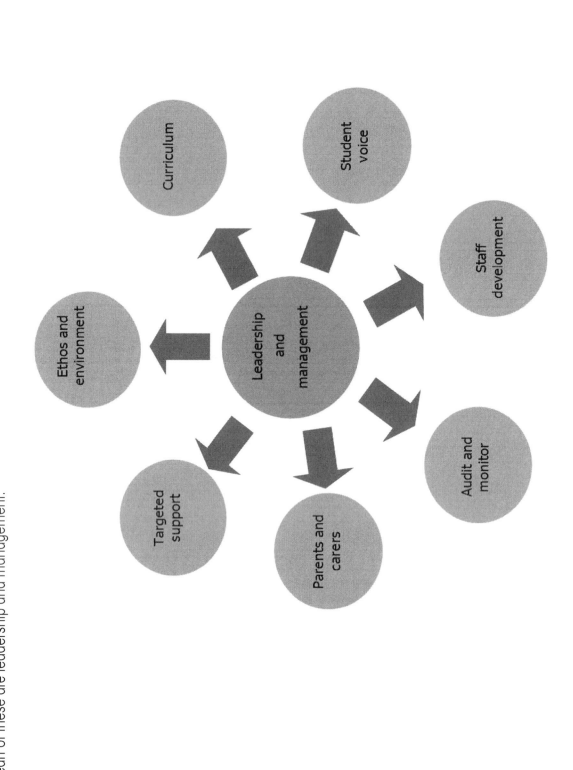

Thinking and finding out

Based on good practice, the following audit tool enables schools to judge how they are developing positive mental health and wellbeing initiatives within their school. For each criterion you can grade your performance as Red, Amber or Green.

RED means that you do not meet any aspects of the criteria used to describe this area.

AMBER means that you partly meet the criteria

GREEN means that you fully meet the criteria.

The first column shows the area being considered, the second column describes what best practice would look like and the final column is for evidence demonstrating the RAG rating you have given.

The 8 areas explored match the 8 key principle areas identified by Public Health England and the Children's and Young People's Mental Health Coalition.

Thinking and finding out

Leadership and management

CRITERIA	BEST PRACTICE	SCHOOL RAG RATING	SCHOOL EVIDENCE
Leadership and management are visibly committed to promoting emotional and mental health and wellbeing within the whole school environment.	1.1 As a school we have a named member of staff from the Senior Leadership Team (SLT) who has overall responsibility for social and emotional health and wellbeing and mental health, and all staff are aware of who this is.		
	1.2 As a school we have a named school Governor who supports policy development and monitors social and emotional health and wellbeing and mental health outcomes.		
	1.3 SLT and the governing body model positive attitudes and behaviours that promote mental health and wellbeing.		
	1.4 Mental health and wellbeing are prominently referenced within school improvement plans, policies and practices (e.g. safeguarding, confidentiality, PSHE, behaviour and rewards, anti-bullying, inclusion, SRE, SEN, health and safety, E Safety, drug and alcohol education, self-harm, equality)		

Thinking and finding out

	1.5 As a school we have a mental health and wellbeing policy in place that clearly sets out how we support children and young people, parents and staff.	1.6 There are a range of systems in place to support staff wellbeing and positive mental health.	1.7 There are opportunities for staff to undergo training on emotional literacy and mental health issues.	1.8 There are systems in place to help staff support each other and contribute to the team.	1.9 Staff feel supported by colleagues in managing difficult day-to-day events.

Overall RAG rating for the area of leadership and management:

Thinking and finding out

Actions required to move this area forward:

Thinking and finding out

School ethos and environment

CRITERIA	BEST PRACTICE	SCHOOL RAG RATING	SCHOOL EVIDENCE
School ethos and environment that demonstrate respect and value diversity	2.1 Stigma associated with mental health problems is challenged		
	2.2 School uses assemblies and special focus days/weeks to explore different areas that impact mental health and wellbeing (anti-bullying week, mental health and wellbeing week, national day of kindness)		
	2.3 The school has an anti-bullying and discrimination culture supported by planned curriculum opportunities.		
	2.4 The school has a range of effective responses if bullying or discrimination occurs.		
	2.5 The school promotes inclusion, connectedness and belonging in a variety of ways amongst staff and children.		

Thinking and finding out

	2.6 Support is available for all members of the school community and is clearly signposted on the website and prospectus. All pupils, parents and staff know what to do if they need to talk to someone.	2.7 Younger children are supported by older children and young people in a variety of ways, both on and off the playground.	2.8 Lunch areas, toilets, playgrounds and corridors are clean and pleasant for staff, children and parents. Children feel safe both inside and on the playground.	2.9 Staff have a clean and comfortable space to relax and to plan and work.

Overall RAG rating for the area of leadership and management:

Thinking and finding out

Actions required to move this area forward:

Thinking and finding out

Curriculum, teaching and learning

CRITERIA	BEST PRACTICE	SCHOOL RAG RATING	SCHOOL EVIDENCE
Curriculum, teaching and learning	3.1 School provides co-ordinated and valued learning opportunities to teach about social and emotional wellbeing and positive mental health through PSHE and SRE as well as through other dedicated curriculum opportunities and activities.		
	3.2 Staff receive appropriate training to support them in delivering positive learning about mental health and wellbeing.		
	3.3 Classroom climates are respectful and participative for all.		
	3.4 Consideration is given to how the individual needs of all children and young people, including vulnerable children, children with special educational needs and disabilities and children with English as an additional language, are met and developed.		
	3.5 All children and young people's achievements, not just academic ones, are celebrated within the school community.		
	3.6 Assessments are carried out in ways that boost children and young people's self-confidence and motivate learning.		

Thinking and finding out

	3.7 Books, posters and resources are on display or available, facilitating discussion of common themes, such as divorce, losing friends, fear, anger and change.		
	3.8 Pupil progress meetings have emotional wellbeing as one of their focus areas. Staff are aware of the procedures to follow when they are concerned about children and young people's emotional wellbeing.		
	3.9 There are suitable resources available for identifying individual and group needs for additional support in developing emotional literacy and social competencies.		
Overall RAG rating for the area of leadership and management:			

Thinking and finding out

Actions required to move this area forward:

Pupil voice

CRITERIA	BEST PRACTICE	SCHOOL RAG RATING	SCHOOL EVIDENCE
Pupil voice	4.1 As a school we ensure that children and young people have the opportunity to express their views and influence decisions on all aspects of school life that affect their mental health and wellbeing. This includes engagement with children at an individual level as well as collectively – for example when developing curriculum activities and content and providing pupil support.		
	4.2 Providing the forums and mechanisms for children and young people to participate, such as School Council, Equalities Team, Wellbeing Champions, Peer Mentoring and Eco Warriors.		
	4.3 The school development plan contains targets that reflect priorities identified by children and young people.		
	4.4 Staff create opportunities to consult with children and young people about their learning.		
	4.5 Opportunities for peer support are maximised.		
	4.6 A whole school assessment on emotional and mental health and wellbeing is undertaken each year, with the data feeding into the provision that is developed to support children and young people.		

Copyright material from Alison Waterhouse (2021), *Wellbeing Champions*, Routledge

Thinking and finding out

Overall RAG rating for the area of leadership and management:	Actions required to move this area forward:

Staff wellbeing and development

CRITERIA	BEST PRACTICE	SCHOOL RAG RATING	SCHOOL EVIDENCE
Staff wellbeing and development	5.1 Staff mental health and wellbeing are highly valued and promoted.		
	5.2 Staff in key roles are suitably trained and engaged in regular supervision.		
	5.3 A range of training opportunities are available to staff, including courses and e-based learning. Staff receive appropriate training to support them in delivering positive learning about social and emotional competencies and mental health and wellbeing.		
	5.4 Staff wellbeing is a key area in all performance management meetings and forms a target for each staff member.		
	5.5 A staff wellbeing policy is in place that clearly indicates how staff are supported within the school and signposts to other outside support.		
	5.6 Staff surveys are conducted once a year to collect staff views, and the data from this are clearly seen within the school development plan.		

Copyright material from Alison Waterhouse (2021), *Wellbeing Champions*, Routledge

Thinking and finding out

Overall RAG rating for the area of leadership and management:	Actions required to move this area forward:

Thinking and finding out

Identifying need and monitoring impact

CRITERIA	BEST PRACTICE	SCHOOL RAG RATING	SCHOOL EVIDENCE
Identifying need and monitoring impact	6.1 Local- and school-level data are accessed, analysed and used to influence practice, provision and training.		
	6.2 Validated assessments are used to assess children and young people's wellbeing each year. The data collected inform how the provision will develop.		
	6.3 Curriculum interventions are evaluated to assess impact and direct how the provision will develop in the future.		
	6.4 The needs of children and young people vulnerable to mental health problems – including those with adverse childhood experiences (ACEs) as well as black minority ethnic (BME) and lesbian, gay, bisexual and transgender (LGBT) young people – are recognised and addressed.		
	6.5 Vulnerable children and young people have a safe place to go at times of difficulty.		
	6.6 The school has effective procedures in place to prevent exclusions for those children at risk.		

Copyright material from Alison Waterhouse (2021), *Wellbeing Champions*, Routledge

Thinking and finding out

	6.7 There are effective working relationships in place with outside agencies.		
	6.8 There are effective systems in place to facilitate collaboration between different agencies in complex cases.		
Overall RAG rating for the area of leadership and management:			
Actions required to move this area forward:			

Working with parents and carers

CRITERIA	BEST PRACTICE	SCHOOL RAG RATING	SCHOOL EVIDENCE
Working with parents and carers	7.1 Parents and carers are regularly provided with accessible information about mental health and wellbeing policies and procedures and how to access services.		
	7.2 Parents and carers are regularly offered opportunities to participate in events at school that will deepen their understanding of mental health and wellbeing and support their parenting and family life.		
	7.3 Parents and carers are involved in all support provided by the school as well as decisions about their child in regard to mental health and wellbeing.		
	7.4 The school provides additional support to families through a range of activities, such as Family Support Work, Parent/Carer Groups and Family Groups.		
	7.5 A range of people from the local community are involved in activities within the school.		
	7.6 Parents feel able to let the school know of home stresses that might be impacting on the learning of their child.		

Thinking and finding out

	7.7 Parents are offered information in an accessible way on how the school is supporting their child's social and emotional wellbeing.	
Overall RAG rating for the area of leadership and management:		
Actions required to move this area forward:		

Thinking and finding out

Targeted support

CRITERIA	BEST PRACTICE	SCHOOL RAG RATING	SCHOOL EVIDENCE
Targeted support	8.1 The school ensures that all children and young people understand where and how they can access help and support both in and outside of school through the use of prominent signposting, posters, internet websites, planners, etc.		
	8.2 All staff are aware of and understand the risk factors for mental health problems and are able to recognise basic warning signs that suggest a child or young person may need help or support.		
	8.3 All staff are aware of the value and importance of listening to children and young people who are in distress and are supported to help a child or young person who approaches them for help whilst maintaining safeguarding procedures.		
	8.4 All staff are aware of when and to whom (e.g. nominated member of staff) a pupil should be referred if mental health and wellbeing problems are escalating or causing concern.		
	8.5 All staff have undergone conflict resolution training to support them in their work repairing relationships with children and young people.		
	8.6 Following an incident staff and young people engage in an enquiring process that is aimed at restoring relationships.		

Copyright material from Alison Waterhouse (2021), *Wellbeing Champions*, Routledge

Thinking and finding out

	8.7 There are formal systems in place whereby structured meetings (i.e. restorctive conferences) can take place and key participants can hear each other's stories and find a mutually acceptable way to repair harm done.	
Overall RAG rating for the area of leadership and management:		
Actions required to move this area forward:		

Thinking and finding out

Mental health and wellbeing questionnaire results

CONTEXT: Mental health and Wellbeing Champions project

Specific objective:

To collect information from teachers, support staff, parents and children and young people in connection with the Mental Health and Wellbeing support the school has in place.

Wellbeing Champions Facilitator:

Support staff:

SLT link person:

Top three things people believe the school does well in relation to mental health and wellbeing

STAFF	PARENTS	CHILDREN						

Copyright material from Alison Waterhouse (2021), *Wellbeing Champions*, Routledge

Thinking and finding out

Three things the school should develop further to support mental health and wellbeing															
CHILDREN															
PARENTS															
STAFF															

Thinking and finding out

Three things the school should improve to better address mental health and wellbeing	CHILDREN														
	PARENTS														
	STAFF														

Thinking and finding out

In Our School We are Looking for...

Amazing People

Who want to help and support others.

We are creating a group of Wellbeing Champions.

Do you want to be one of them?

Thinking and finding out

Wellbeing Champions are young people who care about the mental health of those around them & want to make a difference.

We are recruiting!

Are You....

Passionate about Mental Health & Wellbeing?

Ready to make a difference by helping others?

Want to be involved in new opportunities & create something positive?

Why not come and get involved?

Contact:

Thinking and finding out

Introduction session for staff (P and S)

Time of activity: 45 minutes

Objective
1. To share the proposal to develop Wellbeing Champions with staff
2. To enable staff to fill out the wellbeing questionnaire
3. To collect views on how the school supports MHWB

Resources
Staff questionnaire
Post-it notes
White board and pens
Application forms
Poster
Reference forms

Activity

1. Explain that you want to create a group of WBC that can support other CYP but that can also develop knowledge and understanding about MHWB within the school.
2. Explain that the Wellbeing Champions will be made up of CYP from throughout the school who would like to help others develop positive ways of looking after their mental health and wellbeing.
3. How this is going to work and what they will do hasn't been decided yet because you need the people who are going to become the Wellbeing Champions to help you work this out.
4. Explain that you will be recruiting CYP with different skills, as the work will cover a variety of things. You can give examples if you have some in mind.
5. Explain that the first phase is to gather information about what the school does well and areas it could develop or improve.
6. Share the questionnaires and ask staff to complete theirs.
7. Ask staff to work in groups and list on Post-it notes all the things the school does that support the MHWB of the CYP.
8. Ask them to place the Post-it notes on large sheets of paper with the headings We Do This Well, We Are Developing This, We Could Do This Better and Things We Might Like to Consider for the Future.
9. Explain that when you have collected all the information from the different groups you will feed back the results.
10. Explain that you will be recruiting CYP who are interested in joining the WBC Team. They will be asked to complete an application form.
11. As part of the application process the CYP need to get an adult and a young person to become a referee for them. This can be their parents but could also be a teacher or other member of staff.
12. Explain that when you have looked at the forms you will interview CYP. This will then be followed by a group activity where they will work with other children on a task. After both of these activities have been completed you will let people know who you think can join the group. If they are successful in joining the group, they will work with you, deciding what the children and young people in school need and what they need to learn to be able to help them.
13. All the WBC will have to undertake a range of training activities, including learning what mental health is as well as active listening, problem-solving, restorative practices and looking after their own wellbeing.
14. All children who become WBC will have to attend supervision. Explain what supervision is and how you will ensure that the WBC and the children they support will stay safe emotionally.
15. Share the flow chart so that staff can easily see how children will be supported within the safeguarding framework.
16. Remind staff about the many different ways the school supports MHWB already so that they can see where the WBC will fit in. Explain how you will be able to refer on to other staff or specialists if you need to.
17. Explain that you would really like to work with other staff on this new venture and ask for people to let you know if they would like to help in any way. This can be big or small and can be from across the school community – admin staff, TAs or other teachers.

Copyright material from Alison Waterhouse (2021), Wellbeing Champions, Routledge

Thinking and finding out

Introduction session for parents (P)

Time of activity: 30 minutes

Objective
1. To share the proposal to develop Wellbeing Champions with parents
2. To help parents understand what the role of the WBC could be about and the application process
3. To get parents to complete the wellbeing questionnaire

Resources
Access to the internet "Talking mental health" video by the Anna Freud Centre

Questionnaire
Intervention pyramid
Flow diagram of how CYP can be referred
Application forms

Activity

1. Share the "Talking mental health" video by the Anna Freud Centre (www.youtube.com/watch?v=nCrjevx3-Js&t=190s).
2. Recap that mental health is about our feelings, thinking, emotions and moods. We all know how to look after our physical health, but sometimes we don't know how to look after our mental health and wellbeing.
3. Explain that as a school you are going to create something that can support other CYP. One way you have chosen to do this as a school is to set up a group called the Wellbeing Champions.
4. The Wellbeing Champions will be made up of CYP from years 4–6 who would like to help others develop positive ways of looking after their mental health and wellbeing.
5. How this is going to work and what they will do hasn't been decided yet because you need the people who are going to become the Wellbeing Champions to help you work this out.
6. Introduce the parents' questionnaire and explain that this will be going out to parents over the next week (or date that has been decided). Explain that this is a really important questionnaire that will help you as a school develop the appropriate support for CYP.
7. Explain that you will be recruiting CYP with different skills, as the work will cover a variety of things. You can give examples if you have some in mind: Friendship Mentors, Playground Mentors, Drop-In Group, Peer Mediators, Buddies, etc.
8. Explain that if CYP are interested they need to complete an application form. On the bottom of the application form is a space for parents to sign.
9. As part of the application process the CYP need to get an adult and a young person to become a referee for them. This can be them as parents but could also be a teacher or other member of staff.
10. Explain that when you have looked at the forms you will interview CYP. This will then be followed by a group activity where they will work with other children on a task. After both of these activities have been completed you will let people know who you think can join the group. If they are successful in joining the group, they will work with you, deciding what the children and young people in school need and what they need to learn to be able to help them.
11. All the WBC will have to undertake a range of training activities, including learning what mental health is as well as active listening, problem-solving, restorative practices and looking after our own wellbeing.
12. All children who become WBC will have to attend supervision. Explain what supervision is and how you will ensure that the WBC and the children they support will stay safe emotionally.
13. Share the whole school approach support diagram with parents and explain how you can refer on to other staff or specialists if you need to.
14. Ask for questions.

Introduction

Copyright material from Alison Waterhouse (2021), *Wellbeing Champions*, Routledge

Thinking and finding out

Introduction session for parents (S)

Time of activity: 25 minutes

Objective

1. To share the proposal to develop Wellbeing Champions with parents
2. To help parents understand what the role of the WBC could be about and the application process
3. To share the parents' questionnaire and gain information

Resources

Access to the internet "We all have mental health" video by the Anna Freud Centre

Questionnaire
Intervention pyramid
Flow diagram of how CYP can be referred
Application forms

Activity

Introduction

1. Share the "We all have mental health" video by the Anna Freud Centre (www.youtube.com/watch?v=DxIDKZHW3-E).
2. Recap that mental health is about our feelings, thinking, emotions and moods. We all know how to look after our physical health, but sometimes we don't know how to look after our mental health and wellbeing.
3. Explain that as a school you are going to create a group of Wellbeing Champions that can support other CYP in a variety of ways. Explain that the school is already doing this in a variety of ways. Share the intervention pyramid.
4. Explain that the Wellbeing Champions will be made up of CYP from throughout the school who would like to help others develop positive ways of looking after their mental health and wellbeing.
5. How this is going to work and what they will do hasn't been decided yet because you need the people who are going to become the Wellbeing Champions to help you work this out.
6. Share the questionnaire with parents and explain that you are collecting information from across the whole school community. This information will help you work with the CYP on what they may be able to do and how this can be developed. Share the wish to co-produce with the children and explain why this is so important.
7. Explain that you will be recruiting CYP with different skills, as the work will cover a variety of things. You can give examples if you have some in mind.
8. Explain that if CYP are interested they need to complete an application form. On the bottom of the application form is a space for parents to sign.
9. As part of the application process the CYP need to get an adult and a young person to become a referee for them. This can be them as parents but could also be a teacher or other member of staff.
10. Explain that when you have looked at the forms you will interview CYP. This will then be followed by a group activity where they will work with other children on a task. After both of these activities have been completed you will let people know who you think can join the group. If they are successful in joining the group, they will work with you, deciding what the children and young people in school need and what they need to learn to be able to help them.
11. All the WBC will have to undertake a range of training activities, including learning what mental health is as well as active listening, problem-solving, restorative practices and looking after our own wellbeing.
12. All children who become WBC will have to attend supervision. Explain what supervision is and how you will ensure that the WBC and the children they support will stay safe emotionally.
13. Share the whole school approach support diagram with parents and explain how you can refer on to other staff or specialists if you need to.

Copyright material from Alison Waterhouse (2021), *Wellbeing Champions*, Routledge

Thinking and finding out

Introduction session for assembly (P)

Time of activity: 30 minutes

Objective

1. To help CYP understand what the role of the WBC could be about so that they will apply to be a Wellbeing Champion

Resources

Access to the internet "Talking mental health" video by the Anna Freud Centre

Questionnaire
Intervention pyramid
Flow diagram of how CYP can be referred
Application forms

Activity

Introduction

1. Share the "Talking mental health" video by the Anna Freud Centre (www.youtube.com/watch?v=nCrjevx3-Js&t=190s).
2. Recap that mental health is about our feelings, thinking, emotions and moods. We all know how to look after our physical health, but sometimes we don't know how to look after our mental health and wellbeing.
3. Explain that as a school you are going to create something that can support other CYP. One way you have chosen to do this as a school is to set up a group called the Wellbeing Champions.
4. The Wellbeing Champions will be made up of CYP from years 4–6 who would like to help others develop positive ways of looking after their mental health and wellbeing.
5. How this is going to work and what they will do hasn't been decided yet because you need the people who are going to become the Wellbeing Champions to help you work this out.
6. Help the CYP understand that you need people with different skills, as some may help other CYP and some may write about the work the WB Champions are doing or take photos for the newsletter. Others may create assemblies or support people when they have an argument with someone. Others might want to share information about how to stay mentally healthy. You just don't know until you find out who wants to be in the group and what the school needs.
7. Share the poster they will see around school.
8. If they are interested they need to collect an application form from you and fill it out.
9. As part of the application process they need to get an adult and a young person to become a referee for them. A referee is someone who is willing to fill out a form and share why they think they would make a good WBC. They recommend them. This can be their parents but could also be a teacher or other member of staff.
10. Show them the forms and tell them when they have to hand them in – with their references.
11. Explain that when you have looked at the forms you will ask the people who have applied to come and talk to you – they will have an interview. This will then be followed by a group activity where they will work with other children on a task. After both of these activities have been completed you will let people know who you think can join the group. If they are successful in joining the group, they will work with you, deciding what the children and young people in school need and what they need to learn to be able to help them.

Copyright material from Alison Waterhouse (2021), *Wellbeing Champions*, Routledge

Thinking and finding out

Introduction session for assembly (S)

Time of activity: 30 minutes

Objective

1. To share the proposal to develop Wellbeing Champions with parents
2. To help CYP understand what the role of the WBC could be about so that they will apply to be a Wellbeing Champion

Resources

Access to the internet "We all have mental health" video by the Anna Freud Centre

Application forms

This session can be done as an assembly or as a class-based activity

Activity

1. Share the "We all have mental health" video by the Anna Freud Centre (www.youtube.com/watch?v=DxIDKZHW3-E).
2. Recap that mental health is about our feelings, thinking, emotions and moods. We all know how to look after our physical health, but sometimes we don't know how to look after our mental health and wellbeing.
3. Explain that as a school you are going to create something that can support other CYP. One way you have chosen to do this as a school is to set up a group called the Wellbeing Champions.
4. The Wellbeing Champions will be made up of CYP from throughout the school who would like to help others develop positive ways of looking after their mental health and wellbeing.
5. How this is going to work and what they will do hasn't been decided yet because you need the people who are going to become the Wellbeing Champions to help you work this out.
6. Help the CYP understand that you need people with different skills, as some may help other CYP and some may write about the work the WB Champions are doing or take photos for the newsletter. Others may create assemblies or support people when they have an argument with someone. Others might want to share information about how to stay mentally healthy. You just don't know until you find out who wants to be in the group and what the school needs.
7. Share the poster they will see around school.
8. If they are interested they need to collect an application form from you and fill it out.
9. As part of the application process they need to get an adult and a young person to become a referee for them. A referee is someone who is willing to fill out a form and share why they think they would make a good WBC. They recommend them. This can be their parents but could also be a teacher or other member of staff.
10. Show them the forms and tell them when they have to hand them in – with their references.
11. Explain that when you have looked at the forms you will ask the people who have applied to come and talk to you – they will have an interview. This will then be followed by a group activity where they will work with other children on a task. After both of these activities have been completed you will let people know who you think can join the group. If they are successful in joining the group, they will work with you, deciding what the children and young people in school need and what they need to learn to be able to help them.

Introduction

Wellbeing Champions risk assessment (example P)

WHAT IS THE RISK?	WHAT IS THE IMPACT ON THE PROJECT?	RATING (LIKELIHOOD)	RATING (IMPACT)	WHAT ARE YOU DOING ALREADY?	WHAT ELSE COULD YOU DO TO MANAGE THE RISK?	ACTION BY WHOM?
WBC become upset by the information or conversations they experience.	WBC don't feel able to manage and so choose not to take part. OR Parents become upset and complain to SLT.	Low	Medium	Choice of support chosen to offer Training Supervision Reflective practice 1:1 support	Review recruitment process. Share the WBC role with parents and the work the CYP do at special events and in newsletters.	WBC Facilitator
Children share confidential information with other children.	CYP won't trust the work of the WBC and so will not engage. Children get upset about others knowing something that should be confidential.	Low	High	Robust training and follow-up training sessions Supervision Session records Monitoring of information shared by WBC Facilitator	None	WBC Facilitator
WBC giving unhelpful/ wrong advice	CYP don't feel helped/supported by programme and so no longer use it.	Low	Medium	Robust training Supervision Reflective practice Session records	None	WBC Facilitator

Thinking and finding out

Disclosure by CYP not picked up and raised in supervision by WBC.	Serious safeguarding or mental health need unaddressed.	Low	High	Training Supervision Reflective practice 1:1 support	Buddy system	WBC Facilitator
Wellbeing mentors not given jobs or mentoring with others to undertake.	WBC become disillusioned and stop volunteering.	Low	High	Commitment of WBC Facilitator Supervision Referrals from staff, parents or children	None	WBC Facilitator
WBC Facilitator leaves school or is on long-term sick leave.	WBC are not able to be matched to children with needs. WBC do not have supervision.	Low	High	Ensure WBC Facilitator is not working alone.	None	SLT

Wellbeing Champions risk assessment (example 5)

WHAT IS THE RISK?	WHAT IS THE IMPACT ON THE PROJECT?	RATING (LIKELIHOOD)	RATING (IMPACT)	WHAT ARE YOU DOING ALREADY?	WHAT ELSE COULD YOU DO TO MANAGE THE RISK?	ACTION BY WHOM?
Breach of confidentiality within the WBC project	CYP won't trust the work of the WBC and so will not engage.	Low	High	Robust training and follow-up training sessions Supervision Session records	None	WBC Facilitator
WBC giving unhelpful/wrong advice	CYP don't feel helped/supported by programme and so no longer use it.	Low	Medium	Robust training Supervision Reflective practice Session records	None	WBC Facilitator
Disclosure by CYP not picked up and raised in supervision by WBC.	Serious safeguarding or mental health need unaddressed.	Low	High	Training Supervision Reflective practice 1:1 support	Buddy system	WBC Facilitator
Challenging behaviour in the drop-in sessions	WBC no longer wish to participate. Other CYP no longer come to the drop-in. Complaints from parents/staff.	Medium	Medium	Drop-in is supported and monitored by WBC lead staff. Ground rules are in place. Other site staff are aware of sessions.	Use tutor time to go over the rules with all CYP.	WBC Facilitator
WBC become upset by the information or conversations they experience.	WBC don't feel able to manage and so choose not to take part.	Low	Medium	Training Supervision Reflective practice 1:1 support	Review recruitment process.	WBC Facilitator

Copyright material from Alison Waterhouse (2021), *Wellbeing Champions*, Routledge

Thinking and finding out

Wellbeing Champions risk assessment

WHAT IS THE RISK?	WHAT IS THE IMPACT ON THE PROJECT?	RATING (LIKELIHOOD)	RATING (IMPACT)	WHAT ARE YOU DOING ALREADY?	WHAT ELSE COULD YOU DO TO MANAGE THE RISK?	ACTION BY WHOM?

Thinking and finding out

Action plan example primary

Goal	Measure of Success
To set up a Friendship Bench on the playground for children who have no one to play with or have fallen out with their friends For Friendship Mentors to monitor the bench and help children who go there to play	Children will be seen to use the Friendship Bench and will talk about how much better playtime is now that it is in place and they have peers to talk to and play with.

ACTION STEP	RESOURCES	TRAINING
Step 1: To raise money for a Friendship Bench and put it on the playground with a sign	Friendship Bench and sign cost	N/A
Step 2: To recruit Friendship Mentors to support those children who go to the bench	Badges or tabards for the Friendship Mentors	• To learn a variety of playground games • Active listening • Problem-solving
Step 3: To share how the Friendship Bench will work and what the Friendship Mentors' role is in an assembly	Assembly time Presentation	A practice with the CYP so that they can undertake the assembly and explain their role
Step 4: Meeting with the lunchtime supervisors to explain about the Friendship Bench and how it will work	Time to meet with lunchtime supervisors	A practice with the CYP so that they know what to say
Step 5: Article in the weekly newsletter to share the work of the group with the parents and to explain about the Friendship Bench.	Article for the newsletter	CYP to write the article.
Step 6: Monitor the use of the Friendship Bench and how many children have used it each day.	Clipboard and pens	CYP to understand how to collect the data.
Step 7: Questionnaire at the end of term to collect feedback from the children on friendships on the playground	Questionnaire	CYP to go and talk to classes and hand out the questionnaire. Children to interpret the data.

Thinking and finding out

Action plan example secondary

Goal	Measure of success
To create a drop-in for CYP at lunchtime 4 days of the week	CYP will use the drop-in and engage with the WBC running it. Feedback from CYP after a term will demonstrate that they have found the facility useful.

ACTION STEP	RESOURCES	TRAINING
Step 1: To find a suitable room for the drop-in	Room in school that can be used	N/A
Step 2: To have a range of resources to use in the drop-in	Board games, cards, colouring sheets, pens and pencils, paper and Plasticine Books, comics and magazines	N/A
Step 3: To train the WBC to run the drop-in	Training materials Time to train CYP	• Active listening • Problem-solving • How to play board games • Conflict resolution
Step 4: To share information about the drop-in with the CYP	Assembly time Presentation Email for form tutors Posters around school Paper and art materials for posters	• A practice with the CYP so that they can undertake the assembly and explain their role • Email to tutors • Posters
Step 5: Article in the weekly newsletter to share the drop-in with the parents and to explain why it has been put in place and what it will do	Article for the newsletter	CYP to write the article.
Step 6: Monitor the use of the drop-in and how many children have used it each day.	Record book Supervision	CYP to understand how to collect the data and how to ensure information is recorded to maintain confidentiality.
Step 7: Questionnaire at the end of term to collect feedback from the children on friendships on the playground	Questionnaire	CYP to go and talk to classes and hand out the questionnaire. Children to interpret the data.

Mental health and Wellbeing Champions action plan P/S

Thinking and finding out

CONTEXT:	Success criteria
Specific objective: To create, train and develop a CYP Wellbeing Champions Group to support the development of MHWB throughout the school	◆ ◆ ◆ ◆
Priority leads: **Support staff:** **SLT link person:**	"In order to help their pupils succeed, schools have a role to play in supporting them to be resilient and mentally healthy." (DfE)

SPECIFIC ACTIONS	TRAINING: HOW, WHEN, WHO	RESOURCES – WITH COSTS

Copyright material from Alison Waterhouse (2021), *Wellbeing Champions*, Routledge

Thinking and finding out

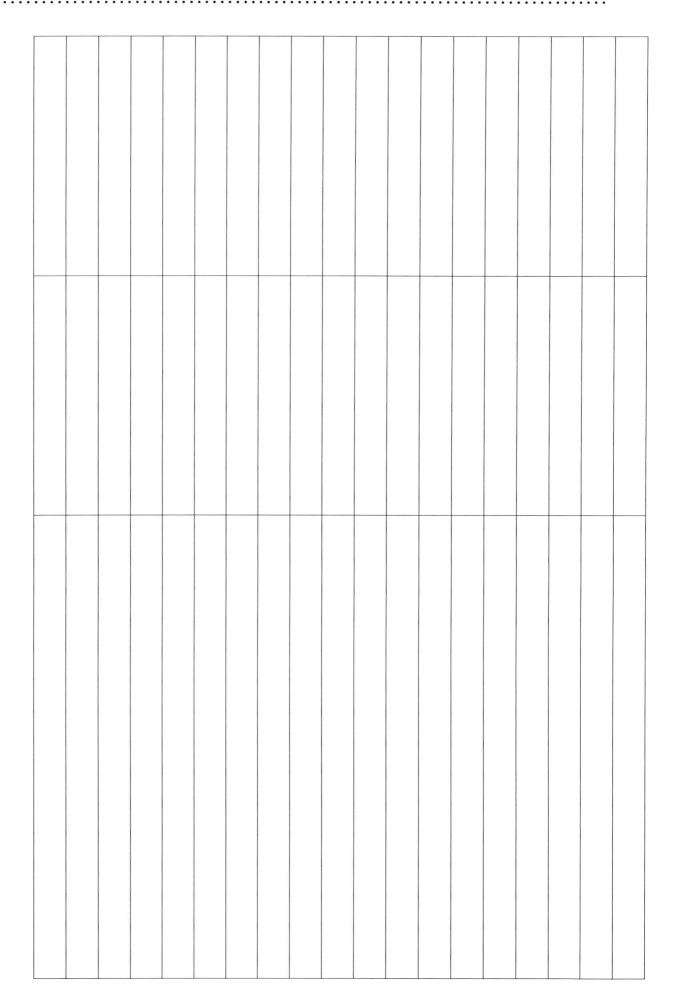

Thinking and finding out

Review

Term:		Date:									Next steps:		Senior leadership feedback (Dated):	
	KEY ACTIONS TAKEN	**IMPACT**												

Thinking and finding out

Action plan

Goal	Measure of success

ACTION STEP	RESOURCES	TRAINING
Step 1:		
Step 2:		
Step 3:		
Step 4:		
Step 5:		
Step 6:		
Step 7:		
Step 8:		
Step 9:		

Proposal documentation for Senior Leadership Team: Wellbeing Champions

DOCUMENTATION	COMMENTS	INCLUDED
Questionnaire results		
List of Wellbeing Champions		
Areas identified and steps to take		
Whole project action plan		
Training schedule		
Risk assessment		
Flow diagram of work to be undertaken		
Safeguarding documentation		
Seven essential elements		

Thinking and finding out

Flow chart for setting up the Wellbeing Champions

Deciding to explore the use of Wellbeing Champions in your school

Look at ways of doing this and then get SLT approval to write a proposal

Undertake the wellbeing survey with CYP, staff and parents

Complete Wellbeing provision pyramid

Identify what school does well, what it could improve and ways the Wellbeing Champions can add to the provision already in place

Recruit Wellbeing Champions so that they can help design the project

First session with WBC team. Share what you have found

Together identify areas that the WBC could undertake/address

Thinking and finding out

```
Together identify training needed and
how this can be delivered
            ↓
Together identify resources needed and
how they would be used
            ↓
With the WBC write the proposal for the
project for the SLT
            ↓
Once SLT agreement has been given
undertake the training
            ↓
Clarify referral routes
            ↓
Share the project and how it will work
with the whole school
            ↓
Set up and run weekly supervision
            ↓
Review
```

Thinking and finding out

How to become a Wellbeing Champion flow chart for CYP

```
┌─────────────────────────────────────┐
│ Be curious: find out what the WBC   │
│ will be doing                        │
└─────────────────────────────────────┘
                  ↓
┌─────────────────────────────────────┐
│ Think about why you want to help    │
│ others and be a WBC                  │
└─────────────────────────────────────┘
                  ↓
┌─────────────────────────────────────┐
│ Fill in application form.            │
└─────────────────────────────────────┘
                  ↓
┌─────────────────────────────────────┐
│ Find another young person and adult │
│ to act as your referee               │
└─────────────────────────────────────┘
                  ↓
┌─────────────────────────────────────┐
│ Attend individual interview          │
└─────────────────────────────────────┘
                  ↓
┌─────────────────────────────────────┐
│ Attend group interview               │
└─────────────────────────────────────┘
                  ↓
┌─────────────────────────────────────┐
│ Wait to hear whether you are        │
│ suitable at this time                │
└─────────────────────────────────────┘
                  ↓
```

Thinking and finding out

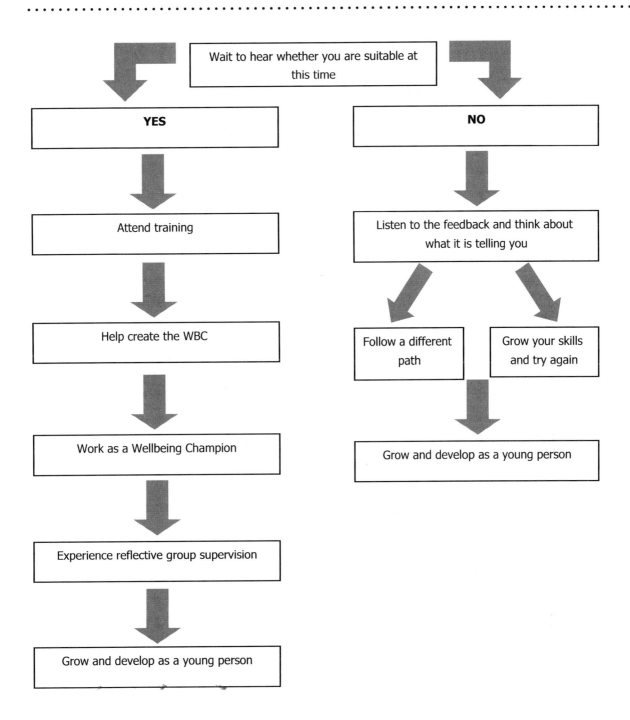

Thinking and finding out

Mental health and wellbeing support pyramid

Tier 1: Core

Foundations for positive mental health and wellbeing which happens throughout the school environment for ALL children and young people.

Tier 2: Supplemental

Small group interventions or support for SOME children and young people.

Tier 1: Intensive

Individual interventions and support to address considerable skill gaps for a few children and young people. These CYP may have EHCP's, BSP's and or receive support from a Mental Health Practitioner.

Thinking and finding out

Wellbeing Champions application form	
School:	**Name:**
Wellbeing Champion Facilitator:	**Gender:**
	Age:
Please answer the following questions in as much detail as possible.	
1. Why would you like to be a Wellbeing Champion?	
2. What qualities and skills do you bring to the Wellbeing Champions role?	
3. Why do you believe this is an important role to develop within your school?	

Thinking and finding out

....

4. What do you enjoy doing when you are not at school?

5. Give the name and contact details of a child and adult who know you well and who can provide you with a reference. The reference will need to share why they think you would be a good Wellbeing Champion and the skills and qualities they believe you have that will enable you to undertake the role within school.

Name of young person:	Name of adult:
Contact details (class):	Contact details:
Date:	Signature:

Wellbeing Champions reference form

Name:
has applied to be a Wellbeing Champion and has given your name as a referee for this role. Please complete the form below, sharing the skills and attitudes this young person has that would make them a suitable candidate for this role in school.

Wellbeing Champion Facilitator:

Please answer the following questions in as much detail as possible.

1. Why do you think this young person would make a positive Wellbeing Champion?

2. What qualities and skills do you believe they would bring to the role of Wellbeing Champions?

Thinking and finding out

3. In what capacity do you know this young person?	
Name of young person:	Name of referee:
Contact details (class):	Contact details:
Date:	Signature:

Thinking and finding out

Flow chart to show how children and young people can be referred

```
Referral to the WBC Facilitator from staff, parents,
Teaching Assistants or other staff working in school. For
secondary schools this may also include CYP
                        ↓
              Referral form completed
                        ↓
WBC Facilitator approaches young person to discuss the
WBC project and see if this is something the CYP would
like. They can share the many different ways the project
can support to find the most suitable
```

Three branches from the above box:

Left branch: Child refuses the support suggested → Wellbeing Champions Facilitator ensures appropriate staff informed

Middle branch: Child agrees to the support → The WBC Facilitator shares the wishes of the CYP with their WBC Team and a suitable Mentor is identified/provision put in place or access arranged → The WBC Facilitator informs parents and seeks agreement if needed → Review of provision by WBC Facilitator

Right branch: Child refuses the support suggested, however agree to something else offered by school → Wellbeing Champions Facilitator ensures support is put in place and appropriate staff informed

Chapter 2

Selection and training

Selection and training

RECRUITING THE WELLBEING CHAMPIONS

There are a variety of different ways to recruit your champions. You can use an assembly to share the work they may be involved in or you can speak to individual classrooms or run a poster campaign. I think assemblies work best, followed by posters letting children and young people know how and when to apply. This also helps in informing staff, letting them know what you are doing and how the WBC project will work. If you work in a secondary school it is also useful to send an email to all the Tutor Groups to let them know what the WBC will be doing and the process for recruitment. They can then help by following up with this information after your assembly, nudging children and young people they feel would make suitable Wellbeing Champions in your direction.

The really important and rather unusual thing to hold in mind is that you are trying to recruit CYP who can help you work out, co-create and decide what the Wellbeing Champions will do and how they will support the other CYP within your school. This is *not* a toolkit that tells you what to do. It is a guide to help you and the CYP within your environment identify what is needed and then create a variety of ways to meet the needs you have all identified. CYP within the school are often best placed to design a programme that can help and support others. This way of working also enables CYP to be proactive in finding a solution for a problem or need. By working alongside a trusted and skilled adult they can develop skills as well as ways of working and thinking that they can then take out into their community or take forward in their own life. The belief and experience of being able to make a difference are very powerful gifts to give to CYP.

A question to think about is what are the skills and attitudes that would be beneficial for your Wellbeing Champions to possess? I would suggest that they need to:

- be enthusiastic
- really want to help others and play a positive part in their community
- be reflective and open to new learning experiences
- enjoy creating positive relationships with peers
- be good listeners

You may also want CYP who have the experience of engaging with peer support themselves or of CYP who have first-hand experience of mental health difficulties. These are both valuable skills and experiences to have access to and can be really helpful for the group to talk about and listen to.

Once you have worked out which recruitment method to use you can get underway. I have always asked CYP to apply for the post of WBC. The process involved helps to emphasise the importance of the role and often causes CYP to talk to family and friends about the project.

Selection and training

APPLICATION FORM

Asking CYP to apply for the WBC role and fill out an application form helps to establish the importance and seriousness of the role. The form needs to ask why the CYP wish to apply for the role, what skills they believe they have that would enable them to be a WBC and why they think the role is a positive one to develop within their school. The application form also needs to have a section for references. This section needs to be completed by a friend or teacher and should state why they believe the candidate would make a good WBC. The form also needs a section for a parent to complete, giving permission for CYP to become a WBC.

Once you have received all your applications forms – don't forget to give a deadline – you can go through them and start to understand the CYP who are interested in the role, why they have applied and the skills they bring. This enables you to start thinking about the training and the needs your CYP may have linked to the focus and roles you have identified as being needed.

INDIVIDUAL INTERVIEW

Following the application comes the interview. I always interview all those CYP who apply, believing that the process itself is of great value to them. It also allows me to ask a variety of questions, and it enables me to think with the CYP as to whether this is really the best role for them and why.

During the interview we talk about the role, the training they will need to undertake and the commitment to the project. The last thing you need is to train a group of CYP, who then decide that supporting other people over lunchtime or during breaks is not something they can do.

The interview process takes about 20 minutes per person. This allows me to write notes on each application after the interview. This information can then be incorporated into a letter to each CYP, asking them to take part or suggesting another route for them to focus on.

GROUP INTERVIEW

Once you have interviewed all CYP who applied for the Champions role you can then invite groups back to undertake a group task. This allows you to observe CYP working together as well as their communication skills and ability to relate to others. If you have CYP you are a little uncertain about, this can be a good opportunity to watch them interact with others and can help you make a final decision.

It is worth saying at this point that a WBC Team works best if it is made up of a variety of CYP. This may involve having CYP as Champions who have needed or would need the support themselves as well as CYP who may have a range of learning differences. This allows you to

101

Selection and training

Group interview (P/S)

Time of activity: 45 minutes

Objective

1. To observe children and young people working together on a group task to understand if they have the skills and abilities to be part of the Wellbeing Champions project.

Resources

Cones—5 per team
Number cards 1-5
Bingo card

Objects for an obstacle course
Headphones
Blindfold
Mask

Activity

1. Congratulate the children and young people for achieving this stage of the interview. Thy have written a really good application form, have undertaken the personal interview which they did well and now it is time for the group interview.
2. Explain that the purpose of the group interview is to allow you to observe them working within a group and seeing the skills that they have when working with others. This includes, active listening, accepting the ideas and views of others, managing time and a range of communication skills.
3. Give the children a Bingo card and explain that you want them to walk around the group and find a person who has done the things on the bingo card. When they have they can cross the square off. The person who gets a line first can call out BINGO.
4. Divide the group up into smaller groups so that each of the groups has 4-6 people.
5. Line each team up and explain that under the cones laid out in a line in front of each team are the numbers 1-5. Their job is to run up to a cone and look at the number. They have to bring the numbers back in the correct order.
6. If the first player runs to the first cone and it has a number 4 under it they must run back empty handed. The next player then runs and looks under a cone of their choice. They can only bring their number back if it is the correct number in the sequence.
7. Divide the children into groups of 4 and explain that they are going to do an obstacle course with a difference as a team. The whole team has to complete the course. Hand out a blindfold, a pair of headphones and a mask (you can use the paper ones that surgeons use) Explain that within each group they need to choose someone who will be blind and wear the blindfold, someone who will be deaf who will wear the headphones and someone who can not speak who will wear the mask. The task is to make sure that all get to the end of the obstacle course safely.
8. Set each group off at different times so that they don't get tangled up.
9. When all have finished, ask each team member to put a hand on the shoulder of someone who really helped them, this could be positive words, physical help, or calming responses.
10. Debrief the children so that they can talk about the experience.
11. Feedback some of the positive things that you have seen and watched them do.

Group interview

Selection and training

gain a much better perspective on the needs of the CYP within your school and how to meet those needs. It also adds a great deal to the training and conversations that happen within this time as well as during weekly supervision sessions.

The group task works best with 4–6 participants and a carefully chosen activity. A range of activities that can be used can be found in the Group Interview.

LETTER OF INVITATION

Once you have interviewed all your applicants and observed them during the group interview it is time to make your choice. It is important to think about how a CYP may feel if they are not accepted. It is hard to receive a letter telling you that you have been unsuccessful in achieving something as an adult, so as a young person this is really difficult if a high proportion of other CYP have been accepted or a particular friend has been accepted. To prevent this from becoming a very negative experience it may be that you decide to use all the CYP who have applied and tailor the training and activities to suit a range of skills, or you may decide to have a face-to-face conversation with those CYP who are not successful before the letters go out to those people who have been successful.

If you choose not to use all the candidates and have a face-to-face conversation you can share the positive skills they displayed and help them think about what they need to do to be successful next time or discuss another area they may be better suited for.

Once you have made your selection you can send out letters inviting CYP to join the WBC Team. Within the letter it is useful to add one or two points as to why they have been chosen. The letter should also contain details of the training as well as when it will be and how it will be undertaken, along with a reminder that a commitment to complete all the training is needed.

TRAINING

The training of the Wellbeing Champions is divided into two very specific sections:

1. Planning and designing the Wellbeing Champions project

   The process of identifying the aspects of supporting CYP the school does well as well as the areas where the school could do better and how forms the core of the work in this section.

2. Training the Wellbeing Champions to deliver the project

   Specific training enabling the CYP to deliver the provision that has been designed forms the core of the work within this section.

Selection and training

*I may not be able to do great things On my own. But I can do little things that make a **BIG** difference to people every day.*

THE IMPORTANCE OF BEGINNINGS AND ENDINGS

Before moving on to the training a quick note needs to be made of the importance of beginnings and endings in all projects. Both are really key to the project working and developing in a positive way.

If we think about beginnings – the beginning of a new term, new group, new job or new baby – they are all merged with hope and optimism. The beginning holds the promise of something new and exciting. However, people who have experienced disappointment and disillusionment that have damaged their sense of hope and excitement tend to have an underlying fear of disappointment. Running alongside hope and the fear of disappointment runs the fear of failure, the fear of not being good enough and the fear of something not working or going wrong.

How you start the work with the CYP will give them a template for their own work with others. Sharing your excitement and your fear will enable them to think about and acknowledge their own.

One thing I have always found to be useful at the beginning of any new venture with CYP is to think together about the expectations of the people involved. To do this I use a triangle, with the children, myself and the organisation at each of the points. We then explore what each hopes/ expects of the other. This then generates discussion, questions and a need to find out. It also helps make all involved be clear about what they need to undertake the role they have chosen.

The last part of this focus is asking what each could do to sabotage the work. This is a vital question, as it introduces the concept of sabotage on a conscious and unconscious level.

Selection and training

When working with people, having an understanding of the way the mind works on both a conscious and nonconsciousness level is vital.

Sabotage is a great concept to share with the CYP, as it allows you to talk openly about the things you might encounter and how you might deal with them in a curious and non-confrontational way. When you ask the question you will probably get a variety of interesting answers. What might the CYP do to sabotage the work? They might be late for meetings, not fill out forms, refuse to follow procedures, etc. It is at this point you can help the CYP understand that if these things start to happen it is a signal that something is not working for that person in some way and so will need to be discussed, explored and reflected on.

It is really interesting to hear what the CYP think you might do to sabotage the work. This may include not listening to their ideas, forgetting to do things, running out of time or changing what has been agreed on without telling them.

Beginnings need to be thought about, planned and carefully organised to enable all people to feel safe and considered. It is important to help the CYP understand that just as you have planned and thought about how to start with them they will need to do the same for the CYP they are going to meet and support in their new role.

Endings are another really important area to pay attention to. We are aware that for some people endings are full of sadness and can trigger a range of feelings, emotions and behaviours. This will be no different for your Wellbeing Champions and the CYP they will support. Helping them to think about endings at each point of the training and to reflect on how they feel will help them mirror this way of working with the CYP they will support. Each section can act as a mini ending before you move on to the next section.

It is often our attitude at the beginning that determines what will happen thereafter.

Selection and training

PHASE 1: PLANNING AND DESIGNING THE WELLBEING CHAMPIONS PROJECT

You should now have collected information on what CYP, staff and parents think the school does really well and what things they would like the school to develop or do better. You also have your own ideas and thoughts about MHWB and how CYP might need or want to be supported, and you have recruited your WBC. It may seem like a strange way to start because you still have no real concrete idea of how the WBC support will develop – you just have the idea, the passion and some people who want to make a difference in your school.

Most training packages tell you what to do and how to do it. I am afraid this one is a bit different, so if that is the sort of package you are looking for, you are in the wrong place. If, however, you are curious and creative and understand that rigid training packages are not always the right way to go for all schools and you want to create something specific for your school environment and the CYP within it, then you are most definitely in the right place.

So what next?

Your next step is to get people together and talk, explore and brainstorm. This is much easier than it may seem on the surface, and there are a range of things you can do to streamline the process. But be warned: whenever you co-produce, things get messy before they get sorted out.

I have always found that it is good to go into the first meeting with the main purpose of getting people acquainted and helping them share what they think they are good at. This may involve talking to people, sharing ideas, problem-solving or creating artwork, to name just a few.

Getting to Know You is Lesson Plan 1 (P is always for primary and S is always for secondary age CYP) and shares how this can be done. The lesson plans are only ideas, so you may want to make them your own by completely rewriting them, or you may want to use bits and pieces. Feel free to choose what is best for your situation, as you know your CYP and your environment best.

Once you have started to create and get to know your group, the second step is to get them to think with you about what you have already found out and what ways you can begin to develop to support and help others. What We Know is the second lesson plan, and it looks at how to share what you have found with the CYP and how to help them start to think about and explore what to do with regard to the needs that have been identified. This stage takes a bit longer, but it is well worth taking the time to explore with the CYP and to tease out what they think and to gather a range of possible ways of meeting the needs identified. Now you have a group that is starting to understand and work together, and you have a range of options and possible ideas for supporting others.

Selection and training

Your next step is to write an action plan. Ready Steady Action is the third lesson plan to undertake with the CYP. When you work on the action plan, you can do this together or with a few CYP who are more interested in supporting this phase. The aim will be to create an action plan you can share with the rest of the group. After everyone has agreed to it, you and the group will then present it to the SLT.

The presentation to the SLT needs to identify the sections the questionnaires highlighted as areas where the school already does well in supporting MHWB and those that staff, children and parents feel could be improved. The presentation will then demonstrate which areas the CYP feel they can develop and how they will go about doing this. It will also highlight what they will do and how and the training and resources they will need. The presentation can be undertaken in a variety of ways: PowerPoint, discussion, presentation or short drama sketches with a narrative. It is a golden opportunity for CYP to put this together and share in the process.

Once the SLT have agreed to the proposal the second phase of the training can be undertaken. During phase 2 the needs and skills identified to undertake the support systems and activities can be explored, taught and practised.

PHASE 2: TRAINING THE WELLBEING CHAMPIONS TO DELIVER THE PROJECT

Now that you have had your action plan agreed to, you can work out the second part of the training schedule. You have to work with the CYP to set up a timetable of activities to show which ones will be put in place first. Many of the training sessions will be important for a variety of activities, so the overlap is good. If the first activity you want to put in place is a Friendship Bench for the playground followed by Peer Mediators, then the training might look like this:

Active listening, body language, communication, playground games, restorative practice

The active listening and body language and communication aspects will all add to the restorative practice.

It is useful to create cards that show the different activities and the training needed so that CYP can choose which areas they would like to support and are clear about which training they will need to do. An example of this might be that some children may want to support others on the playground but not want to do any assemblies or presentations.

The following section includes a range of training sessions. Each school and WBC can therefore pick and choose which training they need and the order in which they are done. They are all individual but can be grouped together to support different areas.

Selection and training

Once you have decided on the order of the activities you wish to put in place with the CYP, you can now start the training. It is really helpful to have some areas that form the foundation of the work, and I would suggest that these are:

- active listening
- communication
- body language
- empathy
- recognising and understanding emotions
- how emotions impact the way we behave
- self-limiting beliefs
- the emotional alarm system
- resolving conflict
- problem-solving

Once you have designed your training schedule you will have an idea about how long the training will take to deliver. It is worth balancing the activities so that you have some that come on line quickly and some that take a bit more time. There is nothing worse for CYP than to sign up to do something and then not be able to do anything for ages whilst they are training.

How you deliver the training is an interesting question that you will need to think about. Do you do this in a block of time or do you do some each week over a half-term/term? This will very much depend on your timetable and when you build in the training time. Most young people won't give up their lunchtimes very often. After school can be a useful time to do the training, as school rooms are more available and you will find that less interruptions happen. If after school is not suitable, you could use drop-down days or off-timetable weeks. It is really up to you to find a time that works best for you and your WBC.

Once you have decided on the times and days and the focus of the training you need to enable you to get specific activities to happen you can fill out the training log sheet and share it with the CYP.

At the beginning of each training session it is really worth exploring with the CYP what they want out of the session and why and how they will know if the training has achieved this for them. See the Training: My Hopes sheet to help you do this. At the end of each training it is useful if the CYP fill out a Training: Feedback sheet. Examples of both of these are at the end of the chapter. The CYP will also need to be given a certificate showing the training they undertook and achieved (see end of chapter).

Learning how is a beautiful art and one that is rarely lost. It is a gift that continues to grow with each new experience.

Selection and training

RESOURCES

Section 1

Initial Session Assembly Primary
Initial Session Assembly Secondary
Recruitment Poster Primary
Recruitment Poster Secondary
Wellbeing Champions Application Form
Wellbeing Champions Reference Form
Interview Questions
Group Interview
Bingo Card
Letter Inviting Candidate for Interview
Letter Declining Candidate for the Post of Wellbeing Champion
Letter to Confirm Wellbeing Champion
Letter to Parents about Wellbeing Champions
Blank Action Plan
Mental Health and Wellbeing Action Plan

Section 2: training part 1 – designing and co-producing the Wellbeing Champions programme

Getting to Know You Primary and Secondary
All About Me Sheet
Hopes, Fears, Expectations Primary and Secondary
Hopes, Fears and Expectations Triangle
What We Know Primary
Opportunities and Ideas Example Primary
What We Know Secondary
Opportunities and Ideas Example Secondary
Ready Steady Action Primary
Ready Steady Action Secondary
Action Plan Example Primary
Action Plan Example Secondary
Action Plan Blank
Mental Health and Wellbeing Action Plan Blank

Selection and training

Section 3: training activities and resources for Wellbeing Champions

1. Active Listening Part 1 Primary
   Active Listening Secondary
   Guide for Active Listening
   Active Listening in Action

2. Active Listening Part 2 Primary
   Active Listening Part 2 Secondary
   Passive List Behaviour
   Active List Behaviour

3. Body Language Primary
   Body Language Secondary
   How We Communicate Pie Chart
   Emotion Words
   Actions

4. The Words We Use Primary
   The Words We Use Secondary

5. Points of View Primary
   Points of View Secondary
   Social Dilemmas

6. Problem-Solving Primary
   Problem-Solving Secondary

7. What is an Emotion Primary and Secondary
   Emotional Story Cube

8. Emotions and Behaviour Primary and Secondary
   Emotional Film Strips Blank
   Box People Pictures

9. Empathy Part 1 Primary and Secondary
   Templates to Design for Friends and Family

10. Empathy Part 2 Primary and Secondary
    Character Cards

Selection and training

11. Emotional Alarm System Primary and Secondary
    Limbic System
    Lateral Surface of the Cerebrum Showing Areas of Functional Localisation

12. Self-Limiting Beliefs Primary and Secondary
    Maisy Label
    Maisy's Day Story
    Labels

13. Self-Limiting Beliefs Part 2 Primary and Secondary
    Fleas in a Jar Picture
    Elephant Picture
    Elephant Story
    A Mind Stretched Saying
    The Belief System Triangle

14. Negativity Bias Primary and Secondary
    Negative Bias Sheet

15. The Bystander Effect Primary and Secondary
    The Impact of Harmdoing on the Harmdoer and the Target
    The Bystander Effect Terminology
    Inhibiting Behaviours

16. Resilience Primary and Secondary
    Book List for Book Tasting on Resilience
    Things That Help Us Keep Going When Life Gets Tough Sheet
    Book Tasting Information
    Menu for Book Tasting

17. Confidentiality Primary and Secondary

18. Let's Talk Mental Health Primary

19. Let's Talk Mental Health Secondary
    Everyday Feelings and Emotions and Overwhelming Feelings and Emotions

20. Respect Primary

21. Respect Secondary

22. Be Your Own Life Coach Primary and Secondary
    Gold Coins

Selection and training

23. Neurodiversity Primary and Secondary
    What is Neurodiversity? Poster

24. Conflict Resolution Part 1 Primary and Secondary
    Method Descriptions
    Restorative and Retributive Justice Descriptions
    Scenarios 1–12

25. Conflict Resolution Part 2 Primary and Secondary
    Ground Rules Prompt
    Restorative Enquiry Script
    Restorative Mediation Prompt Page 1 and Page 2

Section 4

Wellbeing Champions Training Record Sheet
Wellbeing Champions Log Sheet
Wellbeing Champions Certificate
Wellbeing Champions Training Feedback Sheet
Calming Techniques:

- My Favourite Place Primary and Secondary
  My Favourite Place Sheet
- 5, 4, 3, 2, 1 Primary and Secondary
  5, 4, 3, 2, 1 Sheet
- Visualisation Primary and Secondary
  The Beach
  Magic Carpet
  Flying High Like a Butterfly
- Soles of My Feet Primary and Secondary
  Soles of My Feet Sheet

Selection and training

Introduction session/assembly (P)

Time of activity: 25 minutes

Objective

1. To share the proposal to develop Wellbeing Champions with the CYP
2. To help CYP understand what the role could be about so that they will apply to be a Wellbeing Champion

Resources

Access to the internet "Talking mental health" video by the Anna Freud Centre

Application forms

This session can be done as an assembly or as a class-based activity.

Activity

Introduction

1. Share the "Talking mental health" video by the Anna Freud Centre (www.youtube.com/watch?v=nCrjevx3-Js&t=4s).
2. Recap that mental health is about our feelings, thinking, emotions and moods. We all know how to look after our physical health, but sometimes we don't know how to look after our mental health and wellbeing.
3. Explain that as a school you would like to create something that can support other CYP. One way you have chosen to do this as a school is to set up a group called the Wellbeing Champions.
4. The Wellbeing Champions will be made up of CYP from years 4–6 who would like to help others develop positive ways of looking after their mental health and wellbeing.
5. How this is going to work and what they will do hasn't been decided yet because you need the people who are going to become the Wellbeing Champions to help you work this out.
6. Help the CYP understand that you need people with different skills, as some may help other CYP and some may write about the work the WB Champions are doing or take photos for the newsletter. Others may create assemblies or support people when they have had an argument with someone. Others might want to share information about how to stay mentally healthy. You just don't know until you find out who wants to be in the group and what the school needs.
7. Share the poster they will see around school.
8. If they are interested they need to collect an application form from you and fill it out.
9. They need to get an adult and a young person to become a referee for them. A referee is someone who is willing to fill out a form and share why they think they would make a good WBC. They recommend them.
10. Show the forms and tell them when they have to be handed in – with their references.
11. Explain that when you have looked at the forms you will ask people who have applied to come and talk to you – they will have an interview. This will then be followed by a group activity where they will work with other children on a task. After both of these activities have been completed you will let people know who you think can join the group. If they are successful in joining the group, they will work with you, deciding what the children and young people in school need and what they need to learn to be able to help them.

114

Copyright material from Alison Waterhouse (2021), *Wellbeing Champions*, Routledge

Selection and training

Introduction session/assembly (S)

Time of activity: 25 minutes

Objective
1. To share the proposal to develop Wellbeing Champions with the CYP
2. To help CYP understand what the role could be about so that they will apply to be a Wellbeing Champion

Resources
Access to the internet "We all have mental health" video by the Anna Freud Centre

Application forms

This session can be done as an assembly or as a class-based activity.

Activity

1. Share the "We all have mental health" video by the Anna Freud Centre (www.youtube.com/watch?v=DxIDKZHW3-E).
2. Recap that mental health is about our feelings, thinking, emotions and moods. We all know how to look after our physical health, but sometimes we don't know how to look after our mental health and wellbeing.
3. Explain that as a school you would like to create something that can support other CYP. One way you have chosen to do this as a school is to set up a group called the Wellbeing Champions.
4. The Wellbeing Champions will be made up of CYP from throughout the school who would like to help others develop positive ways of looking after their mental health and wellbeing.
5. How this is going to work and what they will do hasn't been decided yet because you need the people who are going to become the Wellbeing Champions to help you work this out.
6. Help the CYP understand that you need people with different skills, as some may help other CYP and some may write about the work the WB Champions are doing or take photos for the newsletter. Others may create assemblies or support people when they have had an argument with someone. Others might want to share information about how to stay mentally healthy. You just don't know until you find out who wants to be in the group and what the school needs.
7. Share the poster they will see around school.
8. If they are interested they need to collect an application form from you and fill it out.
9. They need to get an adult and a young person to become a referee for them. A referee is someone who is willing to fill out a form and share why they think they would make a good WBC. They recommend them.
10. Show the forms and tell them when they have to be handed in – with their references.
11. Explain that when you have looked at the forms you will ask people who have applied to come and talk to you – they will have an interview. This will then be followed by a group activity where they will work with other children on a task. After both of these activities have been completed you will let people know who you think can join the group. If they are successful in joining the group, they will work with you, deciding what the children and young people in school need and what they need to learn to be able to help them.

Introduction

Copyright material from Alison Waterhouse (2021), *Wellbeing Champions*, Routledge

115

Selection and training

In Our School We are Looking for...

Amazing People

Who want to help and support others.

We are creating a group of Wellbeing Champions.

Do you want to be one of them?

Selection and training

Wellbeing Champions are young people who care about the mental health of those around them & want to make a difference.

We are recruiting!

Are You....

Passionate about Mental Health & Wellbeing?

Why not come and get involved?

Ready to make a difference by helping others?

Want to be involved in new opportunities & create something positive?

Contact:

Selection and training

Wellbeing Champions application form	
School:	Name:
Wellbeing Champion Facilitator:	Gender:
	Age:
Please answer the following questions in as much detail as possible.	
1. Why would you like to be a Wellbeing Champion?	
2. What qualities and skills do you bring to the Wellbeing Champions role?	

Selection and training

3. Why do you believe this is an important role to develop within your school?

4. What do you enjoy doing when you are not at school?

5. Give the name and contact details of a child and adult who know you well and who can provide you with a reference. The reference will need to share why they think you would be a good Wellbeing Champion and the skills and qualities they believe you have that will enable you to undertake the role within school.

Name of young person:	Name of adult:
Contact details (class):	Contact details:
Date:	Signature:

Selection and training

Wellbeing Champions reference form

Name:
has applied to be a Wellbeing Champion and has given your name as a referee for this role. Please complete the form below, sharing the skills and attitudes this young person has that would make them a suitable candidate for this role in school.

Wellbeing Champion Facilitator:

Please answer the following questions in as much detail as possible.

1. Why do you think this young person would make a positive Wellbeing Champion?

2. What qualities and skills do you believe they would bring to the role of Wellbeing Champions?

Copyright material from Alison Waterhouse (2021), *Wellbeing Champions*, Routledge

Selection and training

3. In what capacity do you know this young person?

Name of young person:	Name of referee:
Contact details (class):	Contact details:
Date:	Signature:

Copyright material from Alison Waterhouse (2021), *Wellbeing Champions*, Routledge

Selection and training

Group interview (P/S)

Time of activity: 45 minutes

Objective

1. To observe children and young people working together on a group task to understand if they have the skills and abilities to be part of the Wellbeing Champions project

Resources

Cones: 5 per team
Number cards 1–5
Bingo card

Objects for an obstacle course
Headphones
Blindfold
Mask

Activity

1. Congratulate the children and young people for achieving this stage of the interview. They have written a really good application form and have gone through the personal interview, on which they did well, and now it is time for the group interview.
2. Explain that the purpose of the group interview is to allow you to observe them working within a group and see the skills they have when working with others. This includes active listening, accepting the ideas and views of others, managing time and a range of communication skills.
3. Give the children a bingo card and explain that you want them to walk around the group and find a person who has done the things on the bingo card. When they have they can cross the square off. The person who gets a line first can call out "bingo."
4. Divide the group into smaller groups so that each group has 4–6 people.
5. Line each team up and explain that under the cones laid out in a line in front of each team are the numbers 1–5. Their job is to run up to a cone and look at the number. They have to bring the numbers back in the correct order.
6. If the first player runs to the first cone and it has a number 4 under it, they must run back empty-handed. The next player then runs and looks under a cone of their choice. They can only bring their number back if it is the correct number in the sequence.
7. Divide the children into groups of 4 and explain that they are going to do an obstacle course, but with one key difference: the whole team has to complete the course. Hand out a blindfold, a pair of headphones and a mask (you can use the paper ones surgeons use). Explain that within each group they need to choose someone who will be blind and wear the blindfold, someone who will be deaf and wear the headphones and someone who will not be able to speak and will wear the mask. The task is to make sure they all get to the end of the obstacle course safely.
8. Set each group off at different times so they don't get tangled up.
9. When all have finished, ask each team member to put a hand on the shoulder of someone who really helped them. This could be in the form of positive words, physical help or calming responses.
10. Debrief the children so that they can talk about the experience.
11. Discuss some of the positive things you have seen and watched them do.

Group interview

122

Copyright material from Alison Waterhouse (2021), *Wellbeing Champions*, Routledge

Selection and training

Group interview (P/S)

Time of activity: 45 minutes

Objective

1. To observe children and young people working together on a group task to understand if they have the skills and abilities to be part of the Wellbeing Champions project

Resources

Cones: 5 per team
Number cards 1–5
Bingo card

Objects for an obstacle course
Headphones
Blindfold
Mask

Activity

1. Congratulate the children and young people for achieving this stage of the interview. They have written a really good application form and have gone through the personal interview, on which they did well, and now it is time for the group interview.
2. Explain that the purpose of the group interview is to allow you to observe them working within a group and see the skills they have when working with others. This includes active listening, accepting the ideas and views of others, managing time and a range of communication skills.
3. Give the children a bingo card and explain that you want them to walk around the group and find a person who has done the things on the bingo card. When they have they can cross the square off. The person who gets a line first can call out "bingo."
4. Divide the group into smaller groups so that each group has 4–6 people.
5. Line each team up and explain that under the cones laid out in a line in front of each team are the numbers 1–5. Their job is to run up to a cone and look at the number. They have to bring the numbers back in the correct order.
6. If the first player runs to the first cone and it has a number 4 under it, they must run back empty-handed. The next player then runs and looks under a cone of their choice. They can only bring their number back if it is the correct number in the sequence.
7. Divide the children into groups of 4 and explain that they are going to do an obstacle course, but with one key difference: the whole team has to complete the course. Hand out a blindfold, a pair of headphones and a mask (you can use the paper ones surgeons use). Explain that within each group they need to choose someone who will be blind and wear the blindfold, someone who will be deaf and wear the headphones and someone who will not be able to speak and will wear the mask. The task is to make sure they all get to the end of the obstacle course safely.
8. Set each group off at different times so that they don't get tangled up.
9. When all have finished, ask each team member to put a hand on the shoulder of someone who really helped them. This could be in the form of positive words, physical help or calming responses.
10. Debrief the children so that they can talk about the experience.
11. Discuss some of the positive things you have seen and watched them do.

Group interview

Copyright material from Alison Waterhouse (2021), *Wellbeing Champions*, Routledge

Selection and training

GETTING TO KNOW YOU BINGO

Someone who has a pet dog	Someone who has been on holiday to France	Someone who has a middle name that has an "A" in it.	Someone who likes spiders	Someone who is afraid of the dark
Someone who has been to Disneyland	Someone who has ridden a horse	Someone who has been in an aeroplane	Someone who can do a handstand	Someone who can recite the alphabet standing on one leg
Someone who can recite the 5 times table whilst hopping	Someone whose favourite colour is pink	Someone whose birthday is in a month that starts with an "A"	Someone who has broken a bone	Someone who was born in the same month as you
Someone who can whistle	Someone who can sing "Twinkle, twinkle, little star"	Someone who is the youngest in their family	Someone who likes broccoli	Someone who made their bed that morning
Someone who can lick their nose	Someone who can roll their tongue	Someone who has a younger brother or sister	Someone who can knit	Someone who had cereal for breakfast

Selection and training

«Name of school»

«Address1»

«Address2»

«City»

«Post code»

Date:

Dear «Name»

Wellbeing Champions team

Thank you for your application for the above post. I have the great pleasure of inviting you to attend an interview. Please arrive at «Place» (e.g. Main Reception) at «Time» on «Date» and ask for «Contact Person».

The interview will be held with myself and «insert names of other panel members». We ask that you bring a 5-minute presentation to share with the panel, describing why you would like to become a Wellbeing Champion at our school and the skills you possess that would be of benefit. The presentation will be followed by 10 minutes of questions from the panel related to the mental health and wellbeing of children and young people and the role of the Wellbeing Champions.

Please note that it is our intention to read through the two references you supplied with your application and talk to your referees prior to the interview.

I would be grateful if you would confirm whether you will be attending the interview by coming to see me or by leaving a short note for me at Reception. Please let me know if you have any special requirements for the interview.

I look forward to meeting you.

Yours sincerely,

Name
Wellbeing Champions Facilitator

Selection and training

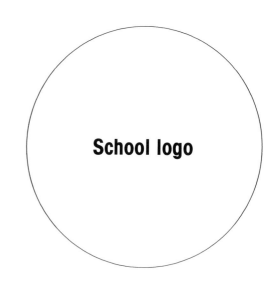

«Name of school»

«Address1»

«City»

«Post code»

Date:

Dear «Name»

Wellbeing Champions

Thank you for your application for the above post. I have the great pleasure of inviting you to attend the next stage of the interview process. The second phase is a group interview. The group interview will take place on «Date» at «Place» (e.g. Class 6) at «Time».

The interview will be held with myself and «insert names of other panel members». The group interview will consist of a group task. During the task we will be observing how all the participants interact, talk and work with each other.

I would be grateful if you would confirm whether you will be attending the group interview by coming to see me or by leaving a short note for me at Reception. Please let me know if you have any special requirements for the interview.

I look forward to working with you.

Yours sincerely,

Name
Wellbeing Champions Facilitator

Selection and training

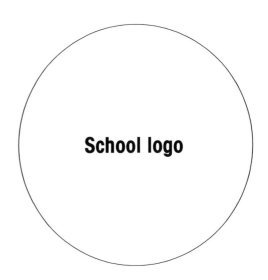

«Name of school»

«Address1»

«City»

«Post code»

Date:

Dear «Name»

Wellbeing Champions

Thank you for your application for the above post. I have the great pleasure of inviting you to attend the next stage of the interview process. The second phase is a group interview. The group interview will take place on «Date» at «Place» (e.g. Class 6) at «Time».

The interview will be held with myself and «insert names of other panel members». The group interview will consist of a group task. During the task we will be observing how all the participants interact, talk and work with each other.

I would be grateful if you would confirm whether you will be attending the group interview by coming to see me or by leaving a short note for me at Reception. Please let me know if you have any special requirements for the interview.

I look forward to working with you.

Yours sincerely,

Name
Wellbeing Champions Facilitator

Selection and training

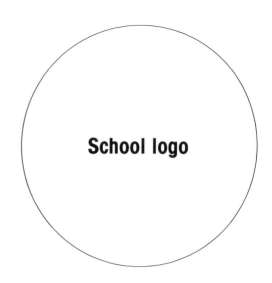

«Name of school»

«Address1»

«City»

«Post code»

Date:

Dear «Name»

Wellbeing Champions

Thank you for your application for the above post. I am writing to you to let you know that, on this occasion, you have not been successful in your application.

Both myself and «names of the other interview panel members» were impressed by «list one aspect of the interview process you were impressed with». However, we feel that «share your reason for not choosing them». We hope that during the next year you can develop these skills so that when we look to recruit new Champions in the future you will apply.

Yours sincerely,

Name
Wellbeing Champions Facilitator

Selection and training

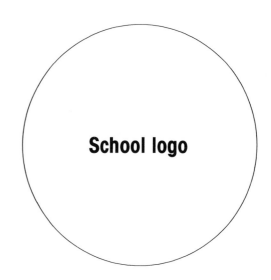

«Name of school»

«Address1»

«City»

«Post code»

Date:

Dear «Name»

Wellbeing Champions

Thank you for your application for the above post. I have the great pleasure of writing to you to let you know that you have been successful in your application. I would therefore like to invite you to become one of the Wellbeing Champions. Both myself and «names of the other interview panel members» were very impressed by «list three aspects of the interview process you were impressed with».

I would be grateful if you would confirm whether you would like to accept this offer with a short letter addressed to me, handed into Reception.

I really look forward to working with you and creating a very special Wellbeing Champions Team for our school.

Yours sincerely,

Name
Wellbeing Champions Facilitator

Selection and training

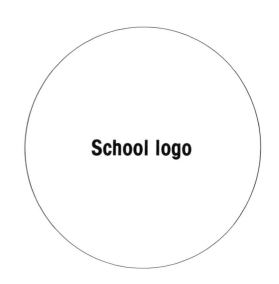

«Name of school»

«Address1»

«Address2»

«City»

«Post code»

Date:

Dear Parents:

Wellbeing Champions

We are in the process of creating a Wellbeing Champions Group within our school. This group will be made up of children from years «name of year groups that can apply». The Wellbeing Champions will be developed by «name of Wellbeing Facilitator», who will work with the children and young people to create this new role. The group will research what school does well and what it could do better in relation to the mental health and wellbeing of children and young people. Members of the group will then work together to identify what sort of support can best meet this need. This will be at a very basic level and will not replace the more professional support that is available. The information they collect and the support they choose to put in place will inform the training that will be required. Co-producing a project with children and young people is a really exciting way of working, so I am delighted that «Wellbeing Champions Facilitator» has chosen to work in this way.

The Wellbeing Champions role is not a replacement for existing support but an addition to the way we work in school. It is also a way of creating a positive ethos within our school in which children and young people are helped to support and think of others.

Selection and training

The Wellbeing Champions will be supervised and supported in helping others by «name of Wellbeing Facilitator». They will share how they will be doing this in the Wellbeing Champions section of our weekly newsletter and on the Wellbeing notice board, which is situated in «place where Wellbeing Champions notice board can be found».

To help develop this new role «name of Wellbeing Facilitator» will conduct an assembly and talk to classes about the role. Children and young people who are interested will be asked to apply by completing an application form. Part of the application form asks for two references, one from an adult and one from another young person. Individual interviews will be held by «name of Wellbeing Facilitator» and will include a presentation about why the young person wishes to be a Wellbeing Champion and why they think mental health and wellbeing are important. After the individual interview there will be a group interview in which children will be asked to undertake an activity together. Those children who are successful will be asked to join the Wellbeing Champions.

We hope you will support your child in taking part in this new venture if they choose to do so. If you have any questions about the role or would like to be involved in any way, please let «Wellbeing Champions Facilitator» know.

Yours sincerely,

Name

Head Teacher

Selection and training

Blank action plan

Goal	Measure of success

Action step	Resources	Training
Step 1:		
Step 2:		
Step 3:		
Step 4:		
Step 5:		
Step 6:		
Step 7:		
Step 8:		
Step 9:		

Selection and training

Mental health and Wellbeing Champions action plan

Context:	Success criteria		
Specific objective: To create, train and develop a CYP Wellbeing Champions Group to support the development of MHWB throughout the school	◆ ◆ ◆ ◆		
Priority leads: **Support staff:** **SLT link person:**	"In order to help their pupils succeed, schools have a role to play in supporting them to be resilient and mentally healthy." (DfE)		
SPECIFIC ACTIONS	**TRAINING: HOW, WHEN, WHO**	**RESOURCES – WITH COSTS**	

Copyright material from Alison Waterhouse (2021), *Wellbeing Champions*, Routledge

Selection and training

Selection and training

REVIEW

Term	KEY ACTIONS TAKEN												Next steps:		Senior leadership feedback (Dated):	
Date:	IMPACT															

Copyright material from Alison Waterhouse (2021), *Wellbeing Champions*, Routledge

Selection and training

Training part 1: designing and co-producing

Training part 1: getting to know you (P/S)

Time of activity: 45 minutes

Objective
To enable the group to get to know each other

Resources
An object of their choosing
Camera

All about Me sheet
Pens, pencils, rubbers, etc.

Activity

1. Ask the CYP prior to the training to bring to the first session an object that says something about them and is something they are happy to share with others. This might be a picture of their dog, a medal they won for swimming, etc.
2. Start the session by reminding the CYP that they have been successful with their application form, their individual interview and their group interview and that you believe they have the ability to become really positive Wellbeing Champions for the school. Today is their first day on this new adventure, so you would like everyone to spend some time getting to know one another as people, including things they like, dislike and enjoy as well as what their passions and talents are.
3. Ask each CYP to start by sharing their object and talking about why it is important to them.
4. You will need to join in, and for some groups you may need to be the person to start.
5. When the CYP have all shared their object, recap the talents and skills you heard about or saw when they spoke. Example: It is clear that, for you to have won the medal you brought, you are obviously prepared to work hard to get something that is important to you *or* It is very easy to see why your dog enjoys your company, as you sound as if thinking about others is very important to you.
6. Hand out the All about Me sheets and explain that you would like them to fill these out, as they will be part of the WBC display in the school and will let people know who they are and a bit about them.
7. Take photos – they can be creative and fun – of the CYP to add to the information and display.
8. Finish the session with a relaxation technique and explain that this is a very good way of allowing them to transition from one space into another. Explain that you will use this technique at the beginning and end of each session.

136

Copyright material from Alison Waterhouse (2021), *Wellbeing Champions*, Routledge

Selection and training

All about me

- **Things I am most proud of..**
- **Subject I enjoy in school......**
- Photo of young person
- **Things I enjoy doing....**
- **My favourite places to go and games to play....**

Selection and training

Training part 1: designing and co-producing

Training part 1: hopes, fears and expectations (P/S) — Time of activity: 45 minutes

Objective
To support the exploration of the hopes, fears and expectations of the CYP for the project

To identify what needs to happen to make it successful for all

Resources
White board and markers

Post-it notes

Pens

Hopes, Fears, Expectations and Triangle

Activity
1. Draw the WBC, Facilitator and Head Triangle and explain that you want to explore with them the hopes, fears and expectations of each group.
2. Ask the children to write on green Post-it notes their hopes for the project. Examples: to enjoy supporting others, to help children feel better about something.
3. Share what they have written and add them to the triangle.
4. Ask the children what their fears are about the project. Ask them to write these on pink Post-it notes. Examples: that I may not know what to do, that I may say the wrong thing and upset someone.
5. Share and discuss. Add to their part of the triangle.
6. Now ask them what they expect from each of the different group members, you as the facilitator and the head of the school. Write these expectations on blue Post-it notes. Examples:
   Facilitator – to be there to help us, to meet us regularly.
   Head – to make sure we have the space to work, to tell others about the work we are doing.
   Each other – to turn up at the sessions, to be positive.
7. Share and discuss.
8. Add expectations to the correct part of the triangle.
9. Ask the children what each group of people could do to sabotage the work. Examples:
   Children – not turn up or help, be late to the meetings, not do what we said we would do.
   Facilitator – be too busy to help us, have to cover other things.
   Head – not be interested in what we do, take the facilitator away.
10. Pose the question, What could we do to stop this?
11. Finish with a relaxation technique to support the children's transition back into class.

Copyright material from Alison Waterhouse (2021), *Wellbeing Champions*, Routledge

Selection and training

Training part 1: what we know (P)

Time of activity: 2 × 45 minutes or 1 × 90 minutes

Objective

To enable the CYP to discuss information from the surveys and questionnaires in relation to what the school does well or areas linked to MHWB that could be developed

Resources

Questionnaire results form
Top 3 areas from each group and section written on cards – 27 cards

A3 paper
Pens, pencils, rubbers, etc.

Activity

1. From the surveys and the whole school audit choose the headlines from each group to share with the CYP. For each group you should have 9 headlines made up of the top 3 things the school does well, the top 3 things the school can continue to develop and the top 3 things the school needs to improve.
2. Write each of these 27 statements on cards. Lay the cards out on tables around the room.
3. Ask the children to read the cards and then share their thoughts about what they have read. Are they surprised? What links can they make? What do the statements make them think of?
4. Take away the cards with the things the school does well and ask the children to share the opportunities the cards offer. Example: I can tell when someone is feeling sad, angry, happy or worried (statement from the CYP questionnaire).
If the group is discussing the 3 things school could improve, what opportunities are there? One of the opportunities might be for class teachers to explore emotions with the children through stories. Another opportunity might be exploring emotions through art.
5. Ask the CYP to write the different opportunities that come from the problems on Post-it notes and stick them around the respective card.
6. Divide the children into groups of 2–4 and give them a card and all the opportunities that have been generated. Ask them to work as a team and pick their top 3 opportunities. Set the cards and the top 3 opportunities identified out on a tables around the room.
7. Ask the children to walk around and read what has been chosen for each card.
8. Give each of the CYP an A3 sheet of paper and ask them to fold it into eighths. Ask them to choose 8 opportunities each and draw an idea for each one in one of the 8 rectangles on the A3 sheet (see example).
9. Discuss and share what they have come up with. Examples:
Teachers explore emotions through stories. Idea – every Friday a Wellbeing Champion visits each class to read a book linked to emotions.
Teachers explore emotions through art. Idea – have an art competition in school with the title "How do I feel?" and display all the pictures in the hall.
10. Ask the children to then choose their favourites from each group. Example: children's group, top 3 areas to improve; best suggestions are . . . .
11. Explain that now they have identified the opportunities each problem offers the school, and they have also identified possible ways of exploring these opportunities. Next time they meet the focus will be on working out which ideas to develop first.

Training part 1: designing and co-producing

Copyright material from Alison Waterhouse (2021), *Wellbeing Champions*, Routledge

Selection and training

OPPORTUNITIES AND IDEAS PRIMARY EXAMPLE SHEET		
CYP group **One of the top 3 things school could improve:** I can tell when someone is feeling sad, angry, happy or worried. **Opportunity:** Teachers to explore emotions using books and stories within the classroom.	**Staff group** **One of the top 3 things school could continue to develop:** I believe I have the knowledge and skills needed to address the emotional wellbeing and mental health of the children and young people I teach/work with. **Opportunity:** Staff training	**Parent group** **One of the top 3 things school could improve:** The school asks for my thoughts, opinions, views and needs about its approach to emotional wellbeing and mental health, and it listens to my voice. **Opportunity:** Ask parents what they think.
	CYP group **One of the top 3 things school could improve:** I can tell when someone is feeling sad, angry, happy or worried. **Opportunity:** Explore emotions through art.	

Selection and training

Training part 1: what we know (S)

Time of activity: 2 × 45 minutes or 1 × 90 minutes

Objective
To enable the CYP to discuss information from the surveys and questionnaires in relation to what school does well or areas linked to MHWB that could be developed

Resources
Questionnaire results form
Top 3 areas from each group and section written on cards – 27 cards

A3 paper
Pens, pencils, rubbers, etc.

Activity

1. From the surveys and the whole school audit choose the headlines from each group to share with the CYP. For each group you should have 9 headlines made up of the top 3 things the school does well, the top 3 things the school can continue to develop and the top 3 things the school needs to improve.
2. Write each of these 27 statements on cards. Lay the cards out on tables around the room.
3. Ask the children to read the cards and then share their thoughts about what they have read. Are they surprised? What links can they make? What do the statements make them think of?
4. Take away the cards with the things the school does well and ask the children to share the opportunities the cards offer. Example: I think my school really cares about me and how I am feeling (statement from the CYP questionnaire).
   If the group is discussing the 3 things school could improve, what opportunities are there? One of the opportunities might be to ask the CYP what they think about school and their learning experience or for the CYP and teachers to be given more time to talk about how they are getting on.
5. Ask the CYP to write the different opportunities that come from the problems on Post-it notes and stick them around the respective card.
6. Divide the children into groups of 2–4 and give them a card and all the opportunities that have been generated. Ask them to work as a team and pick their top 3 opportunities. Set the cards and the top 3 opportunities identified out on tables around the room.
7. Ask the children to walk around and read what has been chosen for each card.
8. Give each of the CYP an A3 sheet of paper and ask them to fold it into eighths. Ask them to choose 8 opportunities each and draw an idea for each one in one of the 8 rectangles on the A3 sheet (see example).w
9. Discuss and share what they have come up with. Examples:
   Ask the CYP what they think about school and their learning experience. Idea – the WBC to visit each form group once a term and conduct a survey.
   Teachers and CYP have more time to talk about how things are going. Idea – for each student to have a meeting with their form tutor or key adult once a term to discuss how they are getting on.
10. Ask the children to then choose their favourites from each group. Example: children's group, top 3 areas to improve; best suggestions are . . . .
11. Explain that now they have identified the opportunities each problem offers the school, and they have also identified possible ways of exploring those opportunities. Next time they meet the focus will be on working out which ideas to develop first.

Training part 1: designing and co-producing

Copyright material from Alison Waterhouse (2021), *Wellbeing Champions*, Routledge

Selection and training

OPPORTUNITIES AND IDEAS SECONDARY EXAMPLE SHEET

CYP group	Staff group	Parents group
One of the top 3 things school could improve: I think my school really cares about me and how I am feeling. **Opportunity:** Ask CYP what they think about school and their learning experience.	**One of the top 3 things school could continue to develop:** I believe I have the knowledge and skills needed to address the emotional wellbeing and mental health of the children and young people I teach/work with. **Opportunity:** Staff training	**One of the top 3 things school could improve:** The school asks for my thoughts, opinions, views and needs about its approach to emotional wellbeing and mental health, and it listens to my voice. **Opportunity:** Ask parents what they think.
	One of the top 3 things school could improve: I think my school really cares about me and how I am feeling. **Opportunity:** Give time to CYP and their form tutor once a term to talk.	

Selection and training

Training part 1: designing and co-producing

Training part 1: ready steady action (P)

Time of activity: 45 minutes

Objective
To enable the CYP to write action plans to support the development of wellbeing initiatives identified from the questionnaires and audit

Resources
Action plan form
Stepping stones

Pens, pencils and paper
Initiatives written on cards

Activity

1. Explain to the CYP that you are going to write an action plan that will set out what you want to do and how. The action plan will then be presented to the SLT by the CYP.
2. Choose one initiative that has been identified as something for the WBC to develop and demonstrate how to set up and write the action plan. Example: to develop a Friendship Bench on the playground.
3. Write the end goal – a Friendship Bench – on a piece of paper and put it on the floor at the far side of the room. Put the word "now" at the other end. Stand the CYP at the "now" end.
4. Lay out the stepping stones from the word "now" to the Friendship Bench.
5. Ask the children to help you work out how to get to the bench – what steps do you need to take?
6. Write their responses on the stepping stones and then move them around if you need to. Once completed you should have an ordered list of what has to be undertaken.
7. Transfer the steps from the stepping stones to the action plan form. See completed action plan form.
8. Help the CYP create the measure of success criteria. Write this on the action plan.
9. Divide the CYP into groups of 2–4 and give them one of the initiatives and a pile of stepping stones. Ask them to write the goal on paper and then set out the stepping stones. Together their job is to create the steps they have to go through to achieve the goal.
10. Once they have completed the stages on the stepping stones ask them to write this on the action plan.
11. Share the different initiatives they have planned and discuss together. Make any changes needed.
12. Finish with a relaxation exercise to help the CYP return to the hustle and bustle of classroom life.

Additional activity:
Ask a small group of Wellbeing Champions to work with you and transfer all the different initiatives onto the overall action plan. Work together and prepare the presentation to the SLT.

Copyright material from Alison Waterhouse (2021), *Wellbeing Champions*, Routledge

Selection and training

Training part 1: ready steady action (S)

Time of activity: 45 minutes

Objective
To enable the CYP to write action plans to support the development of wellbeing initiatives identified from the questionnaires and audit

Resources
Action plan form
Stepping stones

Pens, pencils and paper
Initiatives written on cards

Activity
1. Explain to the CYP that you are going to write an action plan that will set out what you want to do and how. The action plan will then be presented to the SLT by the CYP.
2. Choose one initiative that has been identified as something for the WBC to develop and demonstrate how to set up and write the action plan. Example: to develop a drop-in facility 4 days of the week.
3. Write the end goal – a drop-in facility – on a piece of paper and put it on the floor at the far side of the room. Put the word "now" at the other end. Stand the CYP at the "now" end.
4. Lay out the stepping stones from the word "now" to the drop-in facility.
5. Ask the children to help you work out how to get to the drop-in – what steps do you need to take?
6. Write their responses on the stepping stones and then move them around if you need to. Once completed you should have an ordered list of what has to be undertaken.
7. Transfer the steps from the stepping stones to the action plan form. See completed action plan form.
8. Help the CYP create the measure of success criteria. Write this on the action plan.
9. Divide the CYP into groups of 2–4 and give them one of the initiatives and a pile of stepping stones. Ask them to write the goal on paper and then set out the stepping stones. Together their job is to create the steps they have to go through to achieve the goal.
10. Once they have completed the stages on the stepping stones ask them to write this on the action plan.
11. Share the different initiatives they have planned and discuss together. Make any changes needed.
12. Finish with a relaxation exercise to help the CYP return to the hustle and bustle of classroom life.

Additional activity:
Ask a small group of Wellbeing Champions to work with you and transfer all the different initiatives onto the overall action plan. Work together and prepare the presentation to the SLT.

Training part 1: designing and co-producing

Action plan example primary

Goal	Measure of success
To set up a Friendship Bench on the playground for children who have no one to play with or have fallen out with their friends. For Friendship Mentors to monitor the bench and help children who go there to play.	Children will be seen to use the Friendship Bench and will talk about how much better playtime is now that it is in place and they have peers to talk to and to play with.

ACTION STEP	RESOURCES	TRAINING
Step 1: To raise money for a Friendship Bench and put it on the playground with a sign	Friendship Bench and sign cost	N/A
Step 2: To recruit Friendship Mentors to support those children who go to the bench	Badges or tabards for the Friendship Mentors	• To learn a variety of playground games • Active listening • Problem-solving
Step 3: To share how the Friendship Bench will work and what the Friendship Mentors' role is in an assembly	An assembly time Presentation	A practice with the CYP so that they can undertake the assembly and explain their role
Step 4: Meeting with the lunchtime supervisors to explain about the Friendship Bench and how it will work	Time to meet with lunchtime supervisors	A practice with the CYP so that they know what to say
Step 5: Article in the weekly newsletter to share the work of the group with the parents and to explain about the Friendship Bench	Article for the newsletter	CYP to write the article.
Step 6: Monitor the use of the Friendship Bench and how many children have used it each day	Clipboard and pens	CYP to understand how to collect the data.
Step 7: Questionnaire at the end of term to collect feedback from the children on friendships on the playground	Questionnaire	CYP to go and talk to the classes and hand out the questionnaire. Children to interpret the data.

Selection and training

Action plan example secondary

Goal	Measure of success
To create a drop-in for CYP over lunchtime 4 days of the week.	CYP will use the drop-in and engage with the WBC that are running it. Feedback from CYP after a term will demonstrate that they have found the facility useful.

ACTION STEP	RESOURCES	TRAINING
Step 1: To find a suitable room for the drop-in	Room in school that can be used	N/A
Step 2: To have a range of resources to use in the drop-in	Board games, cards, colouring sheets, pens and pencils, paper and Plasticine Books, comics and magazines	N/A
Step 3: To train the WBC to run the drop-in	Training materials Time to train CYP	• Active listening • Problem-solving • How to play board games • Conflict resolution
Step 4: To share information about the drop-in with the CYP	An assembly time Presentation Email for form tutors Posters around school Paper and art materials for posters	• A practice with the CYP so that they can undertake the assembly and explain their role • Email to tutors • Posters
Step 5: Article in the weekly newsletter to share the drop-in with the parents and to explain why it has been put in place and what it will do	Article for the newsletter	CYP to write the article.
Step 6: Monitor the use of the drop-in and how many children have used it each day.	Record book Supervision	CYP to understand how to collect the data and how to ensure information is recorded to maintain confidentiality.
Step 7: Questionnaire at the end of term to collect feedback from the children on friendships on the playground	Questionnaire	CYP to go and talk to the classes and hand out the questionnaire. Children to interpret the data.

Selection and training

Action plan

Goal	Measure of success

ACTION STEP	RESOURCES	TRAINING
Step 1:		
Step 2:		
Step 3:		
Step 4:		
Step 5:		
Step 6:		
Step 7:		
Step 8:		
Step 9:		

Selection and training

Mental health and Wellbeing Champions action plan

Context:

Success criteria
- ◆
- ◆
- ◆
- ◆

Specific objective:
To create, train and develop a CYP Wellbeing Champions Group to support the development of MHWB throughout the school

Priority leads:
Support staff:
SLT link person:

"In order to help their pupils succeed; schools have a role to play in supporting them to be resilient and mentally healthy." (DfE)

SPECIFIC ACTIONS	TRAINING: HOW, WHEN, WHO	RESOURCES – WITH COSTS						

Copyright material from Alison Waterhouse (2021), *Wellbeing Champions*, Routledge

Selection and training

Selection and training

REVIEW

Term:			Date:											
Key actions taken	Impact													

Next steps:

Senior leadership feedback (Dated):

Selection and training

Training part 2: active listening (P)

Time of activity: 45 minutes

Objective

To be able to listen to another person, giving them their whole attention

To be able to demonstrate some of the active listening skills of paraphrasing and not interrupting or adding own points of view

Resources

Active Listening Highlights sheet

Pens, A3 paper, pencils, etc.
Lined paper

Activity

1. Demonstrate two people engaging in a conversation where the listener is distracted and not listening fully.
2. Discuss how the person talking is feeling.
3. Share with the children that you are going to actively listen to the person and ask them to "spot the difference."
4. Write a list of differences or things the children noticed.
5. Ask the children to get into pairs and try out both active listening and poor listening.
6. Discuss how it feels.
7. Highlight the skills and behaviours used when actively listening to someone.
8. Ask the children to work in groups and create a poster to show how to actively listen to someone.
9. Ask different groups to act out the active listening skills and get the group to record how many skills they use or the number of each skill they use.
10. Discuss as a group how being completely listened to makes you feel and the struggles the person doing this has to manage. Examples: not interrupting, not sharing similar experiences, not offering advice.
11. Finish with a calming relaxation exercise to help the children return to the busy classroom or school.

Training part 2: basic skills

Copyright material from Alison Waterhouse (2021), *Wellbeing Champions*, Routledge

Selection and training

Training part 2: active listening (S)

Time of activity: 45 minutes

Objective

To be able to listen to another person, giving them their whole attention

To be able to demonstrate some of the active listening skills of paraphrasing and not interrupting or adding own points of view

Resources

Active Listening Highlights sheet

Pens, A3 paper, pencils, etc.

Lined paper

Active listening in action: phone conversation

Activity

1. Demonstrate two people engaging in a conversation where the listener is distracted and not listening fully.
2. Discuss how the person talking is feeling.
3. Share with the children that you are going to actively listen to the person and ask them to "spot the difference."
4. Write a list of differences or things the children noticed.
5. Ask the children to get into pairs and try out both active listening and poor listening. Stop and ask the children to demonstrate differences as they are seen.
6. Discuss together how it feels to be truly listened to and when the listener isn't really interested.
7. Ask the children to write/text a conversation on the phone between themselves and their best friend to show the language they would use to support their friend in managing a difficulty.
8. Share the phone conversation as an example and explore the different language used and how this influences the conversation.
9. Highlight the neutrality of the friend throughout. Discuss how hard this is but also how it helped, enabling the person to work through their anger to a place where they had worked out what to do by themselves.
10. Ask the children to work in pairs. Discuss the sorts of scenarios they could use – keep them simple – and ask them to come up with a phone script of their own.
11. Share and discuss.
12. Discuss the times the CYP think they may use this skill as a WBC.
13. Finish with a relaxation exercise to support the return of the CYP to a busy classroom.

Training part 2: basic skills

GUIDE FOR ACTIVE LISTENING

1. Make eye contact when the other person is talking. Most of the time you should aim for eye contact to be about 60% to 70% of the time you are listening.

2. Lean towards the other person and nod your head occasionally. This shows that you are interested and paying attention to what they are saying.

3. Avoid folding your arms, as this body language signals that you are not listening – you shut people out with your folded arms.

4. Instead of joining in the conversation and saying what you think or feel, simply paraphrase what has been said. You might start this off by saying, "In other words, what you are saying is . . ."

5. Do not interrupt whilst the other person is speaking.

6. Do not think or plan what you are going to say in response to their words. This ensures that if they say something at the end you have listened and taken this in – they may change their mind at the end of a conversation or add something important that you may miss if you have an answer ready.

7. In addition to listening to what is said, watch their non-verbal actions. These will give you clues about what they are thinking or feeling as they talk. Non-verbal actions are facial expressions, tone of voice, head movements, hand movements and posture. These can sometimes tell you more than words alone.

8. Whilst listening, stop your own thoughts and internal talk and avoid switching off or daydreaming. It is impossible to attentively listen to someone else and your own internal voice at the same time.

9. Show interest by asking them questions to clarify or help you understand what they are saying. Try and ask open-ended questions to encourage them to share more about what they are thinking or feeling. Try to avoid questions that need only a yes or no answer, as these tend to make the conversation stop or lose flow.

10. Try not to change what you are talking about, as this makes the other person think you are not listening to what they are saying or that you are not interested in their ideas or views.

11. As you listen, be open to what they are saying, listen properly to their ideas and views and try to be neutral and withhold judgement about what they are saying.

Selection and training

ACTIVE LISTENING IN ACTION

The following conversation shows how active listening can make the speaker feel heard and understood and how it helps them to open up and say more about what they think and feel and the reasons behind what they are thinking.

Sally: Hi, Emma. I'm so sorry to phone you like this, but I've had a fight with my sister and I'm feeling really miserable, as we haven't spoken since.

Emma: Hi, Sally. No worries. It's fine. I'm glad you thought you could phone me. It's not a problem. So you had a fight and now you guys aren't talking to each other?

Sally: Yes, we were arguing because I wanted to borrow her long black coat, as I was going out and it looks so good. She'd said I could borrow it, but then she said she had to wear it, as she was going out with Roger. I was so cross, as I was really looking forward to wearing it and I haven't got a decent coat, as Mum said she was getting me one for my birthday next month. It was so unfair, especially as she has said yes, and then just because of that stupid Roger she changed her mind. I got really mad and shouted at her and then slammed out, but now I feel bad. I said some really mean things at the time.

Emma: I hear you. You got really mad about her saying you couldn't borrow her coat when she had said you could, and you shouted and got really angry and said some unkind things, but now you feel bad about it.

Sally: Yes, she just made me so angry, assuming that my going out wasn't as important as her date. She knew I hadn't got a coat, as I had to wait for my birthday. I know her date with Roger was important, but I thought she would keep her word, as she had said I could wear it. I got so cross we couldn't talk about it anymore.

Emma: Sounds like you were angry because she went back on what she had said.

Sally: Totally. Maybe I should just tell her in a calm way how hurt and upset I was and that I know it is her coat, but it was the breaking of a promise that upset me. I just don't like the fact that she is not talking to me, as we normally get on so well and have a real laugh. She probably needs to know I am sorry for what I said and am sorry I got so angry with her – it's only a coat!

Emma: So . . . maybe you will talk to her and tell her you understand her feelings . . . and that you miss talking and sharing things with her.

Sally: Yes, that's what I think I will do. Thanks! I feel a lot better just having a chance to share what I was feeling.

Selection and training

Training part 2: active listening part 2 (P)

Time of activity: 45 minutes

7. Divide the group into pairs and ask each pair to show a short sketch showing listening to someone in a passive way, and then, when you call out "change," turn this into active listening.
8. Finish with a calming relaxation exercise to help the children return to the busy classroom or school.

Training part 2: active listening part 2

Objective

To be able to listen to another person, giving them their whole attention

To be able to demonstrate some of the active listening skills of paraphrasing and not interrupting or adding own points of view

Resources

Passive listening behaviours

Active listening behaviours

iPad

Activity

1. Create a short video with either an adult or a few children showing active listening and passive listening mixed together.
2. Share the video with the children and ask them to work in pairs and write down active listening and passive listening behaviours on Post-it notes as they watch. Put one behaviour on each Post-it note.
3. Create a table on the board labelled Active Listening Behaviours and Passive Listening Behaviours.
4. Ask the children to place the Post-it note labels they have written in the correct column.
5. Discuss what you have found. Rewind the video so that the children can see the behaviours again. Add any that were not seen the first time.
6. Discuss how the person speaking feels when the listener is actively listening and when they are passively listening.

Training part 2: basic skills

Copyright material from Alison Waterhouse (2021), *Wellbeing Champions*, Routledge

Selection and training

Training part 2: active listening part 2 (S)

Time of activity: 45 minutes

Objective

To be able to listen to another person, giving them their whole attention

To be able to demonstrate some of the active listening skills of paraphrasing and not interrupting or adding own points of view

Resources

Passive listening behaviours

Active listening behaviours

iPad

Activity

1. Ask the children to work in pairs and research passive listening behaviour and active listening behaviour.
2. Ask each pair to show a short sketch showing listening to someone in a passive way, and then, when you call out "change," turn this into active listening.
3. Ask the audience to watch for active listening behaviours and passive listening behaviours and to record them on Post-it notes.
4. Divide the board into two columns: Active Listening Behaviours and Passive Listening Behaviours. After each group has had a chance to play ask them to stick their Post-it notes on the correct side of the board.
5. Share how understanding these different types of behaviours may be important to their role of a WBC.

Training part 2: basic skills

Active listening behaviours	Passive listening behaviours
Paraphrasing to show understanding	Looking away from the person talking
Non-verbal cues that show understanding, such as nodding, eye contact, leaning forward	Non-verbal clues that show disinterest, such as leaning back, arms folded, body turned away from speaker
Brief verbal affirmations like "I see," "I know," "Sure," "Thank you," "I understand"	Fiddling with hands or other object
Summarising what the person has said to show you heard them and understood	Not showing understanding of the speaker, just listening and saying nothing
Showing understanding of what the speaker is saying	No involvement with what the speaker is saying
Avoiding distracting gestures or fiddling with objects	Passive facial expressions that convey a lack of engagement
Not interrupting the speaker	Checking phone
Asking questions to show interest	
Facial expressions that show interest	

Selection and training

Training part 2: body language (P)

Time of activity: 45 minutes

Objective

To understand that body language and facial expressions are forms of communication

To be able to identify simple facial expressions and link them with an emotion/feeling

Resources

Birds video clip (www.youtube.com/watch?v=lK13SW0QW04)

A3 paper, pens, etc.

Non-verbal communication video clip (www.youtube.com/watch?v=csaYYpXBCZg)

iPad

"How do I feel" charades

"How we communicate" pie chart

Activity

1. Show the children the birds video clip.
2. Discuss what the birds were feeling and why.
3. How do they know? There were no words spoken.
4. Discuss body language. What is it?
5. Ask the children to give some examples using their bodies to send a message or feeling and using their face to share an emotion.
6. Watch the non-verbal communication video clip and discuss.
7. Ask the children to imagine that the class had a visitor from another planet – the alien has no idea about body language. Ask the children to work in pairs to create a Top 10 Tips list for understanding body language. This can be a poster or a YouTube video post.
8. Share the posters/video and explore which things are hard to understand and why.
9. Play "How do I feel" charades. Cut up the tasks, fold them and put them in a container. Do the same with the emotions, putting them in a different container. Ask a child to take one piece of paper from each container and act out the task in the way the emotion tells them to – this could be hanging out the wash in an angry way.

   The other children have to guess the emotion and the task.
10. Discuss why understanding body language and facial expressions is an important skill for the WBC to understand.
11. Finish with a relaxation exercise before the children return to class

Training part 2: basic skills

Selection and training

Training part 2: body language (S)

Time of activity: 45 minutes

Objective
To understand that body language and facial expressions are forms of communication
To be able to identify simple facial expressions and link them with an emotion/feeling

Resources
Mr Bean shopping trip video clip (www.youtube.com/watch?v=6IlPvYGex2s)
A3 paper, pens, etc.

Non-verbal communication video clip (www.youtube.com/watch?v=csaYYpXBCZg)
Tactics for reading body language video clip (www.youtube.com/watch?v=Nmp_-JByPaY)

Activity
1. Watch the Mr Bean shopping trip video clip.
2. Discuss how we know what is happening when so little is said.
3. Explore and discuss body language.
4. Watch the non-verbal communication and tactics for reading body language video clips.
5. Ask the children to work in pairs and use the skills they have discussed on non-verbal communication to demonstrate listening to a friend talk about something they enjoy.
6. Share the short presentations. Ask the other children to count how many different non-verbal ways of communicating they saw.
7. Pose the question, Why is understanding body language and facial expressions an important skill for the WBC to know?
8. Play "How do I feel" charades. Cut up the tasks, fold them and put them in a container. Do the same with the emotions, putting them in a different container. Ask a child to take one piece of paper from each container and then act out the task in the way the emotion tells them to – this could be hanging out the wash in an angry way. The other children have to guess the emotion and the task.
9. Finish with a relaxation exercise before the children return to class.

Training part 2: basic skills

Copyright material from Alison Waterhouse (2021), *Wellbeing Champions*, Routledge

Selection and training

How we communicate pie chart

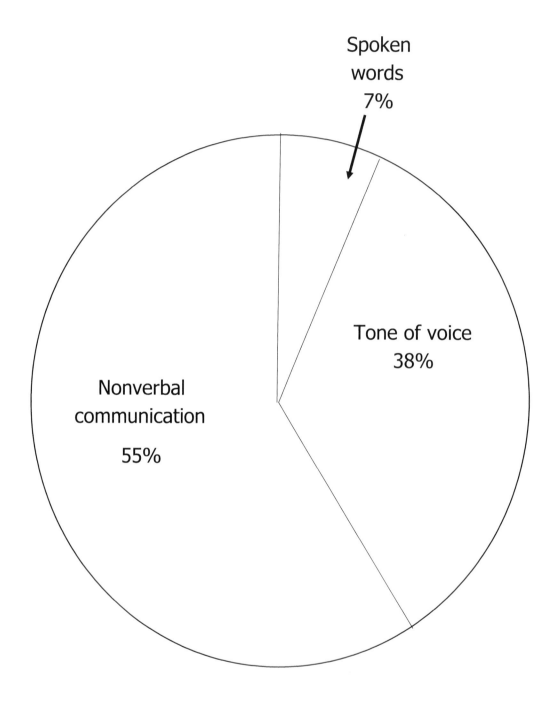

Sad	Excited
Angry	Frustrated
Frightened	Hysterical
Worried	Thoughtful
Miserable	Disgusted
Frantic	Bored
Distracted	Panic
Calm	Cheerfully
Curiously	Impatiently
Irritated	Carefree
Bewildered	Anxious
Rage	Embarrassed

Selection and training

Manic	Tired
Carefully	Furious
Washing up	Making the bed
Washing the car	Hoovering the floor
Making dinner	Ironing
Eating dinner	Having a shower
Doing homework	Mowing the lawn
Dusting	Walking to the shops
Reading a book	Driving a car
Shopping	Digging the garden

Selection and training

Training part 2: the words we use (P)

Time of activity: 45 minutes

Objective

To understand that the language we use is only part of what we communicate to others

To understand that the language we use can be very powerful

Resources

Phileas's Fortune by Agnes de Lestrade and Valeria Docampo

Speeches by famous people

Motivational phrases or cards

Motivational speech video clip (www.youtube.com/watch?v=DjCLbtUOL3A)

Greatest speeches in history video clip (www.artofmanliness.com/articles/the-35-greatest-speeches-in-history/)

Activity

1. Read the children *Phileas's Fortune* by Agnes de Lestrade and Valeria Docampo.
2. Discuss the importance of words.
3. Place a line on the floor and space the numbers 1–10 equally along the line.
4. Ask the children to stand on the line to show how they feel about the statement "Words are just words; they hold no power."
5. Ask each child to explain why they have stood where they have and to give an example to back up their belief.
6. Share important speeches with the children – Martin Luther King, Churchill, etc.
7. Discuss how they make us feel.
8. Share with the children some motivational or thoughtful phrases and ask them to choose one for a friend. Create a special postcard with the words on the card.
9. Discuss why listening to the words people use might support them in their role as a WBC.
10. Pose the question, How might your words support the person who has come to you for help?
11. Finish with a calming relaxation exercise to help the children return to the busy classroom or school.

Training part 2: basic skills

Copyright material from Alison Waterhouse (2021), *Wellbeing Champions*, Routledge

Selection and training

Training part 2: the words we use (S)

Time of activity: 45 minutes

Objective

To understand that the language we use is only part of what we communicate to others

To understand that the language we use can be very powerful

Resources

Motivational phrases or cards
Paper and pens
Motivational speech video clip (www.youtube.com/watch?v=DjCLbtUOL3A)

Greatest speeches in history video clip (www.artofmanliness.com/articles/the-35-greatest-speeches-in-history/)

Activity

1. Place a line on the floor and space the numbers 1–10 equally along the line.
2. Ask the children to stand on the line to show how they feel about the statement "Words are just words; they hold no power."
3. Ask each child to explain why they have stood where they have and to give an example to back up their belief.
4. Share important speeches with the children – Martin Luther King, Churchill, etc.
5. Discuss how they make us feel.
6. Ask the young people to create two short radio plays showing an interaction between two friends. Play 1 has to show the interaction when one is using words badly. Play 2 shows what happens when they both try to use words wisely.
7. Share with the children some motivational or thoughtful phrases and ask them to choose one for a friend. Create a special postcard with the words on the card.
8. Come up with a phrase that promotes thinking about the words we use with each other in the classroom.
9. Discuss why listening to the words people use might support them in their role as a WBC.
10. Pose the question, How might your words support the person who has come to you for help?
11. Finish with a calming relaxation exercise to help the children return to the busy classroom or school.

Training part 2: basic skills

Selection and training

Training part 2: points of view (P)

Time of activity: 45 minutes

Objective

To understand that different people can see and experience things in a different way

Resources

A Tale of Two Beasts by Fiona Roberton

Character masks for your chosen book

Activity

1. Share a well-known story with the children. "Hansel and Gretel" works well.
2. Ask the children to get into small groups and give each person a character from the story – dad, stepmum, witch, Hansel, Gretel. One person needs to be the interviewer.
3. It is useful to make masks for this, as it helps the children get into character.
4. Ask the children to work as a team to come up with questions the interviewer might ask the characters.
   Examples:
   Gretel – How did you feel when you went into the woods?
   Hansel – How did you feel when you knew your father had gone home and left you in the woods?
   Dad – How did you feel when your new wife suggested that you leave the children in the woods as you didn't have enough food to feed them?
   Stepmum – How did it feel to have so little money that you couldn't feed your family?
5. Act out the interview, with the interviewer asking the different characters the questions.
6. Discuss the fact that each of the characters experienced the events differently. They all had different points of view.
7. Share the book *A Tale of Two Beasts* by Fiona Roberton. When you have finished reading it to the children pose the question, Who was lying? Discuss if anyone was actually lying or if they were just telling the story from their point of view.
8. Why does an understanding that different people have different experiences of an event help them as WBC?
9. Finish the session with a relaxation activity to support them in transitioning back into school life.

Training part 2: basic skills

Copyright material from Alison Waterhouse (2021), *Wellbeing Champions*, Routledge

Selection and training

Training part 2: points of view (S)

Time of activity: 45 minutes

Objective
To understand that different people can see and experience things in a different way

Resources
Social dilemma situations

Activity
1. Share the social dilemmas with the children and discuss the characters.
2. Divide the class into groups and give each group the dilemmas. Ask the groups to choose one person to play each of the characters.
3. Ask the groups to create a sketch that shows how the different characters are feeling and what they are thinking. This could be focussed on meetings between different people or an interview with the papers or TV.
4. Share the different sketches and discuss what the children have found/noticed/questioned.
5. What might they take away from this activity that will help them in their role as WBC?
6. Explore the fact that each person has a different point of view and a different understanding of the situation.
7. Finish with a relaxation exercise before the children return to class.

Training part 2: basic skills

Selection and training

Social dilemmas	
The local school keeps getting broken into and vandalised.	**A group of young people keep shoplifting in the local corner shop.**
Caretaker: Mr Smith is very fed up, as he is having to clear everything up and he isn't able to get on with the jobs he needs to.	Mrs George works in the shop and keeps being blamed by the owners for not catching who is stealing from them.
Older lady who lives opposite the school: Mrs Silver is in her 80s and lives alone now that her husband has died. She is frightened by the noises she hears at night and by the stories she reads about in the local paper.	Mr and Mrs Shilling own the shop and have worked hard to get it well established and making money, as they are supporting their two daughters who are at university. They are thinking of closing the shop.
Teenagers – Colin, Tam, Pete and Nim all live near the school and like to meet up outside the corner shop and have a laugh. People keep treating them as if it is they who keep vandalising the school.	Bob, Shane, Raj and a few other teenagers are all part of a group that dares each other to steal from the shop. They think it is funny.
Ted and Chaz are two teenagers who have been excluded from the school, as the school is not able to meet their needs and they have been violent towards other children and staff. They are angry with the school and have been breaking in to wind people up.	Dan, Mark and Digby all go to the shop on their way home from school. They don't like the fact that they are always being watched and feel like people think they are the thieves. They have now stopped going to the shop but have found another one down the road.
Mr and Mrs Stevens own the corner shop and get on well with the teenagers, as their son often hangs out with them.	Ted Oliver is an elderly gentleman in his 90s. He has been visiting the corner shop since he was a young boy and uses it every day as a way of talking to and meeting people. He gets very lonely since his wife died.
Mrs Frant is the head of the school. She is cross that the school keeps getting broken into and vandalised. She and her staff have worked hard to create a good environment for the children, and the vandalisation is costing the school money that they want to spend on other things.	Mrs Webster is the owner of Shop Video, a business that sells and maintains shop video cameras. She has just been asked to install 4 cameras in the corner shop.
PC Becker is the local policeman who is trying to make sure the school is kept safe and who wants to catch the people who are causing so much trouble in the area.	

Selection and training

Training part 2: problem-solving (P)

Time of activity: 45 minutes

Objective

To be able to listen and think about a problem and then generate ideas to solve the problem before exploring each one to find the right solution

Resources

"Dust buddies" short film (www.youtube.com/watch?v=mZ6eeAjgSZI&index=1&list=PLMizheSITLyBew_HdwzzPFS3X7PBQRbL)

Paper, pens, etc.

Activity

1. Explain to the children that you need them to solve a problem, and they need to work together to generate ideas and then choose the best one to do the job.
2. They need to be the problem solvers.
3. Watch the short film "Dust buddies."
4. Stop the film before the dust buddy starts to show how he will get his friend out of the hoover.
5. Ask the children to work in pairs and generate 3 solutions to the problem.
6. Ask the children to choose one solution and write the next part of the story.
7. Ask the children to share their stories.
8. Watch the end of "Dust buddies."
9. What did they think?
10. Ask why they think problem-solving is a good skill for the WBC to develop.
11. Explore the concept of "stealing someone else's learning." This happens when we give people the answers to problems rather than help them come up with a variety of ways to solve the problem for themselves and then choose the right one for them at the time.
12. Finish with a calming relaxation exercise to help the children return to the busy classroom or school.

Training part 2: basic skills

Copyright material from Alison Waterhouse (2021), *Wellbeing Champions*, Routledge

Selection and training

Training part 2: problem-solving (S)

Time of activity: 45 minutes

Objective

To be able to listen and think about a problem and then generate ideas to solve the problem before exploring each one to find the right solution

Resources

The Island by Armin Greder
Paper and pens

Large sheets of paper
Marker pens
Post-it notes

Activity

1. Share the book *The Island* by Armin Greder with the children and then explore what the different problems are that can be found in the story. Examples: What should happen to the stranger? Who should look after the stranger? What if other strangers come? May strangers not be safe to have in the community?
2. The type of problem determines what solution is needed. Ask the children to work in pairs or small groups and explore together one of the problems identified and generate some possible solutions.
    For example, a man has been washed up on the beach. Problem solutions: take him in and look after him, send him back out to sea, lock him up, kill him.
3. Share the different problems and solutions.
4. Which solution is chosen depends on how you think about the stranger. How things are thought about depends on your experience and your culture/family/community.
5. Ask the children to come up with some of the problems they think other CYP may ask them about in their role as WBC.
6. Discuss the possible solutions to the problems.
7. How can the WBC support the CYP who have approached them to find a range of solutions to their own problems?
8. Introduce the concept of "stealing someone else's learning." This can happen if we solve problems for others. We steal their chance of learning how to problem-solve and also the experience of successfully doing this. This is likely to mean that they may always need support with problems.
9. Challenge the WBC to come up with a short sketch to show how to support someone in coming up with a range of their own solutions to a problem. Ask each group to come up with a problem they might meet as a WBC. Write this down and then pass it on to the next group.
10. Share the sketches and discuss the language and phrases they have come up with.
11. Collect the different phrases they like so that they have a bank of them to use when working.
12. Finish with a calming relaxation exercise to help the children return to the busy classroom or school.

Training part 2: basic skills

Copyright material from Alison Waterhouse (2021), *Wellbeing Champions*, Routledge

169

Selection and training

Training part 2: what is an emotion? (P/S)

Time of activity: 45 minutes

Objective

To identify a range of emotions and describe how they make the body feel

To be able to describe an event that may have caused an emotion

Resources

Sad Book by Michael Rosen
A variety of coloured felt pens/crayons

Paper
Plasticine
Pictures of people showing emotions
Emotions story cube

Activity

1. Show the children a range of pictures of people showing emotions.
2. Ask them to describe the emotions – e.g. furrowed brow, downturned mouth, eyebrows pointing inwards towards the nose, angry.
3. Divide the children into groups of 4–6 and put different pictures of people experiencing different emotions on the table. The box people photos could also be used.
4. Ask the children to put the coloured felt pens/crayons that go with each emotion on each picture.
5. Share the colour ranges the children have come up with and discuss why they chose them.
6. Discuss the shapes that might go with different emotions.
7. Read *Sad Book* by Michael Rosen and look at the colours and pictures.
8. Ask the children to say what might have happened to cause the person or box person to feel the emotions they have identified.
9. Ask the children to create a model that goes with one emotion using Plasticine or other clay.
10. Use the emotions dice to create a small group story together.
11. Explore how being able to recognise a range of emotions might be useful to a Wellbeing Champion.
12. Ask the children in groups to write down as many emotions as they can in 2 minutes. Share the different ones they have.
13. Finish with a calming exercise to support the children in returning to the busy school environment.

Training part 2: basic skills

Selection and training

Emotions Dice

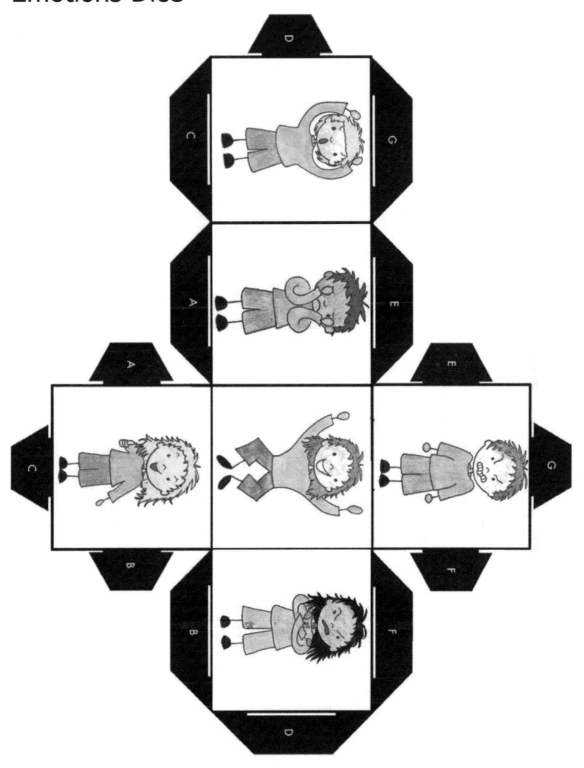

Selection and training

Training part: what is an emotion? P(P)
Time of activity: 45 minutes

Objective
To identify a range of emotions and describe how they make the body feel
To be able to describe an event that may have caused an emotion

Resources
Sad Book by Michael Rosen
A variety of coloured felt pens/crayons

Paper
Plasticine
Pictures of people showing emotions
Emotions story cube

Activity
1. Show the children a range of pictures of people showing emotions.
2. Ask them to describe the emotions – e.g. furrowed brow, downturned mouth, eyebrows pointing inwards towards the nose, angry.
3. Divide the children into groups of 4–6 and put different pictures of people experiencing different emotions on the table.
4. Ask the children to put the coloured felt pens/crayons that go with each emotion on each picture.
5. Share the colour ranges the children have come up with and discuss why they chose them.
6. Discuss the shapes that might go with different emotions.
7. Read *Sad Book* by Michael Rosen and look at the colours and pictures.
8. Ask the children to create a model that goes with one emotion using Plasticine or other clay.
9. Use the emotions dice to create a small group story together.
10. Explore how being able to recognise a range of emotions might be useful to a Wellbeing Champion.
11. Ask the children in groups to write down as many emotions as they can in 2 minutes. Share the different ones they have.
12. Finish with a calming exercise to support the children in returning to the busy school environment.

Training part 2: basic skills

172 Copyright material from Alison Waterhouse (2021), *Wellbeing Champions*, Routledge

Selection and training

Training part 2: emotions and behaviour (P/S)

Time of activity: 45 minutes

Objective
To understand that emotions affect our behaviour and that we can choose how we would like to respond to situations

Resources
- *Wave* by Suzy Lee
- Film clips of waves, rough and calm seas
- Emotional pictures
- Pens, pencils and rubbers
- Paper cut into strips
- Emotional film strips
- *The Island* by Armin Greder
- Box people pictures

Activity

1. Read *Wave* by Suzy Lee (KS2) or *The Island* by Armin Greder (KS3).
2. What emotions and feelings are portrayed in the chosen book?
3. When do the CYP think the amygdala (emotional alarm in the brain) kicked in? What was the reason and the response?
4. Ask the CYP to work in pairs. Give them an emotions film strip and an emotions picture. Ask them to place the picture in the middle space on the film strip. Ask them to think about what may have happened before the picture and after.
5. Share their stories.
6. What is the emotion dependent upon, the thinking brain or the prefrontal cortex (PFC)?
7. Ask the CYP to choose a film strip and fill in what happens before and after.
8. Explore what we may want to do – behaviour affected by our emotions, the amygdala hijacking our thinking brain – and what we can choose to do. Can the CYP relate an example of when they have experienced a strong or big feeling? What did they do? What might they have done differently? Would this change the consequences?
9. Watch a video clip of a wave and link this to the feelings of an emotion. Ask the CYP to work in groups of 4–6 and choose one emotion and come up with all the words they can think of that are linked. Ask them to write the words on small pieces of paper. Example: angry – mad, cross, furious, tetchy, fuming, etc. Now ask them to rank the words from the strongest to the weakest. Lay out the word ladders on the table and ask the CYP to walk around and look at them. If they can add new words, ask them to do so.
   Discuss Dr Jill Bolte Taylor's 90-second rule. She found that the chemicals released by the body that create the emotions we feel last for only 90 seconds. If we can learn to "ride the wave of emotions" and not get caught up in the cognitive – i.e. thinking about them – they will pass.
10. Discuss how knowing about emotions and behaviour might help the CYP in their role as WBC.
11. Finish with a calming relaxation exercise to help the CYP move back into the busy life of school.

Training part 2: basic skills

Copyright material from Alison Waterhouse (2021), *Wellbeing Champions*, Routledge

Selection and training

Training part 2: active listening (P)

Time of activity: 45 minutes

Objective

To be able to listen to another person, giving them their whole attention

To be able to demonstrate some of the active listening skills of paraphrasing and not interrupting or adding own points of view

Resources

Active Listening Highlights sheet

Pens, A3 paper, pencils, etc.
Lined paper

Activity

1. Demonstrate two people engaging in a conversation where the listener is distracted and not listening fully.
2. Discuss how the person talking is feeling.
3. Share with the children that you are going to actively listen to the person and ask them to "spot the difference."
4. Write a list of differences or things the children noticed.
5. Ask the children to get into pairs and try out both active listening and poor listening.
6. Discuss how it feels.
7. Highlight the skills and behaviours used when actively listening to someone.
8. Ask the children to work in groups and create a poster to show how to actively listen to someone.
9. Ask different groups to act out the active listening skills and get the group to record how many skills they use or the number of each skill they use.
10. Discuss as a group how being completely listened to makes you feel and the struggles the person doing this has to manage. Examples: not interrupting, not sharing similar experiences, not offering advice.
11. Finish with a calming relaxation exercise to help the children return to the busy classroom or school.

Training part 2: basic skills

Copyright material from Alison Waterhouse (2021), *Wellbeing Champions*, Routledge

Selection and training

175

Selection and training

Selection and training

Selection and training

Training part 2: empathy part 1 (P/S)

Time of activity: 45 minutes

Objective
To investigate how we learn to empathise with others and understand how they are feeling

Resources
Mirror neurons part 1 video clip (www.youtube.com/watch?v=XzMqPYfeA-s)

Mirror neurons part 2 video clip (www.youtube.com/watch?v=xmEsGQ3JmKg)

T-shirt template, hat template, cup template and pencil case template

Activity
1. Share the video clips on mirror neurons and discuss.
2. Link back to the work on body language and interactions with others.
3. Discuss why empathy is such an important skill to have.
4. Discuss what you might give a friend/family member that would reflect what they like or need – T-shirt, cap, cup, pencil case – and how you could design it just for them. Example: your dad might like BBQs, so you might put hot dogs on his T-shirt.
5. Discuss how this skill of empathising with another could be a helpful skill for the WBC to develop.
6. Explore different scenarios with the children.
7. Finish the session by sharing the different artwork they have developed for a friend or family member.
8. Close the session with a relaxation exercise to enable a smooth transition back into the busy life of school.

Training part 2: basic skills

Selection and training

Templates to design for Friends and Family

Selection and training

Selection and training

Selection and training

Selection and training

Training part 2: empathy part 2 (P/S)

Time of activity: 45 minutes

Objective
To think about another person and identify what they might like or need

Resources
Character cards

A variety of pictures of people in different or difficult situations

Activity
1. Share a variety of pictures with the CYP of different people and discuss what they might be feeling and what they could do to help; e.g. a street cleaner in the rain – a flask of tea.
2. Put the CYP into groups of 4–6 and ask them to choose a card from the character pack and then create 3 magic stars for wishes they might like to make; e.g. a dog – a bone, a walk or to sleep on the children's bed.
3. When the CYP have finished their stars, ask them to share who they chose and what wishes they gave them.
4. At the end of the session ask the CYP to share what went well (WWW) for them and why they think this ability to see and think about someone else and what they are feeling, as well as being able to think of something they need, is important.
5. Ask the CYP what they think the next step is that needs to happen. For example: Step 1: See and understand how someone might be feeling. Step 2: Be able to think about what they need. Step 3: Have the courage or motivation to do something.
6. Explore with the children what obstacles might get in the way of step 3. Examples: no time, do not want other people to see them, don't know what it might lead to, fear, embarrassment.
7. Now help the CYP think about how they could overcome these obstacles. What other ways could they help? How could they offer the help in a different way? For example, they see a young person at school who is upset, but they are on their way to a maths lesson and they have already gotten a warning this week for being late. How could they still help? Tell the office on their way by, ask a friend to tell the teacher why they are late, etc.
8. Finish with a relaxation exercise before the CYP return to class.

Training part 2: basic skills

Copyright material from Alison Waterhouse (2021), *Wellbeing Champions*, Routledge

183

Selection and training

Dog	Postman	Nurse
Lollipop person	Receptionist	Head teacher
Hamster	Wild birds	Ant
Ducks	Chimney sweep	Rubbish bin collector
Gardener	Vet	Farmer
Teacher	Canteen staff	Bank manager
Rain forest	Elephant	The ocean

Selection and training

The prime minister	England's football team	A newborn baby
Indian tiger	African rhino	The Queen
Our school	Your house	Your family
Father Christmas	The Tooth Fairy	The Easter Bunny
Planet Earth	Taxi driver	Fireman
Bus driver	Policeman	A YouTuber
Superman	Mario	Pikachu

Selection and training

Training part 2: basic skills

Training part 2: emotional alarm system (P/S)

Time of activity: 45 minutes

Objective
To understand how our mind and body work to protect us

Resources
The fight, flight, freeze response video clip (www.youtube.com/watch?v=jEHwB1PG_-Q)
Model of a brain and brain picture

The limbic system "Why do we lose control of our emotions?" video clip (https://www.youtube.com/watch?v=3bKuoH8CkFc&t=65s)

Activity
1. Watch the fight, flight, freeze response video clip with the CYP and discuss how the body and mind keep us safe.
2. Ask the CYP to share times when they were aware their alarm system had been triggered. How did they feel?
3. Explore a model of the brain and show them where the limbic system can be found and what it is made up of – hypothalamus, amygdala, thalamus, hippocampus. A good way to remember this is to think of a hippopotamus wearing a hat.
Hypothalamus Amygdala Thalamus Hippocampus
4. Watch the "Why do we lose control of our emotions?" video clip and discuss the concept of "flipping our lid" and the hand model of the brain.
5. Discuss how knowing how the brain works can help us as individuals. How can it support their work as WBC?
6. Ask the CYP to work in pairs and discuss a time when their alarm systems were triggered. Ask them to record on Post-it notes what helped them to cool off and calm down and what made things worse. Use Post-it notes of different colours to reflect cooling off or getting worse.
7. Gather the group and share what they have found. Link back to their work as WBC.
8. Finish with a relaxation exercise before the CYP return to class.

Important points:
The amygdala is an almond-shaped structure in the brain; its name comes from the Greek word for "almond." As with most other brain structures, you actually have two amygdalae. Each amygdala is located close to the hippocampus, in the frontal portion of the temporal lobe.

Your amygdalae are essential to your ability to feel certain emotions and to perceive them in other people. This includes fear and the many changes it causes in the body. If you are being followed at night by a suspect-looking individual and your heart is pounding, chances are that your amygdalae are very active!

Our brain looks for rewards or threats. If it sees a threat it releases chemicals to help us manage that threat. It gets us ready to fight, flee, freeze or flock. The chemicals it releases are cortisol and adrenalin.

If our brain sees a reward – something we like – it releases serotonin and dopamine. These are the pleasure chemicals.

Our emotional brain will often hijack our thinking brain. Our behaviour can sometimes get us into trouble because of this.

Copyright material from Alison Waterhouse (2021), *Wellbeing Champions*, Routledge

The limbic system

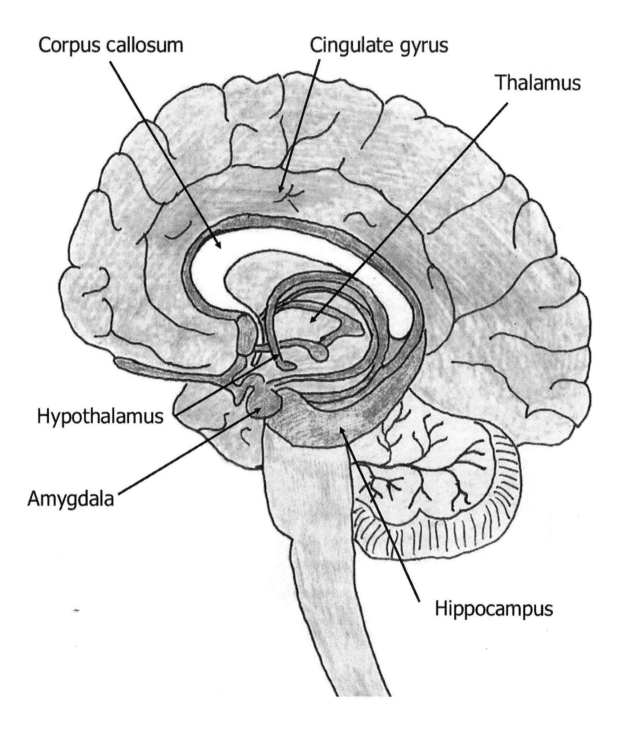

Selection and training

Lateral surface of the cerebrum showing areas of functional localisation

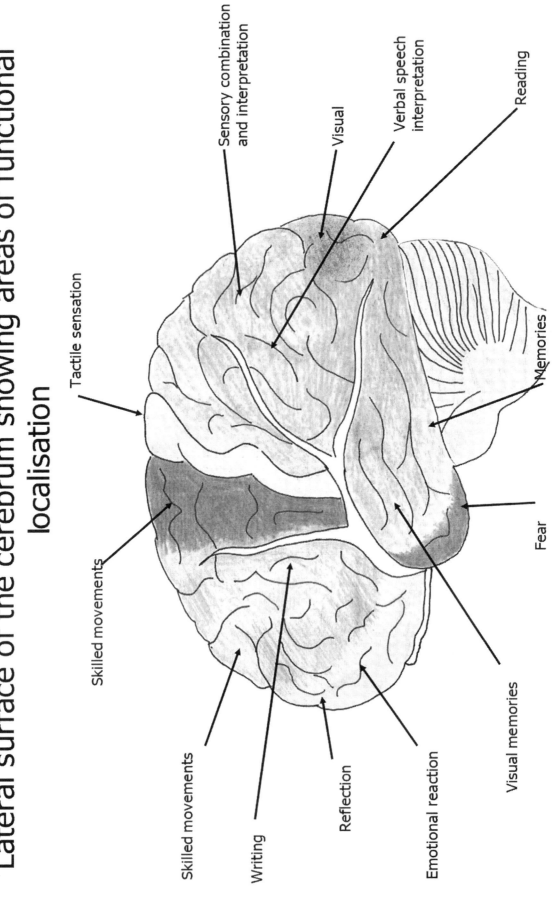

Selection and training

Training part: self-limiting beliefs (P/S)

Time of activity: 45 minutes

Objective

To develop a greater understanding of how we decide what to believe about ourselves

Resources

"Maisy's day" story labels
Post-it notes

Maisy name plate

Activity

1. Share the story "Maisy's day" with the young people.
2. In pairs, ask them to write on a Post-it note all the labels Maisy is given that day.
3. Divide the pile up into positive and negative labels.
4. Ask the CYP to work in pairs and to share a label they have been given. Ask them to explore what they think about this label. Is it true? Would they like it to be? Do they like it or not?
5. Demonstrate with Maisy's picture that the labels can be taken off if she doesn't want them.
6. Ask the young people to come up with 4 labels they would like to collect over the year ahead.
7. In pairs, discuss what they can do or how they can work to collect the labels.
8. Introduce the concept of self-esteem – what we believe about ourselves from the evidence we have gathered (in the form of labels) from how people respond to us.
9. Ask the CYP how they would like the people they meet and work with as WBC to feel. List the words and actions that could make them feel this way.

   That they are important – this could be felt by being listened to.

   That what they feel is important – this might be given by active listening.

   That they are worthwhile – this may be experienced by someone taking the time to chat and talk to them.
10. Finish with a calming relaxation exercise to help the CYP return to the busy classroom or school.

Training part 2: basic skills

Copyright material from Alison Waterhouse (2021), *Wellbeing Champions*, Routledge

Selection and training

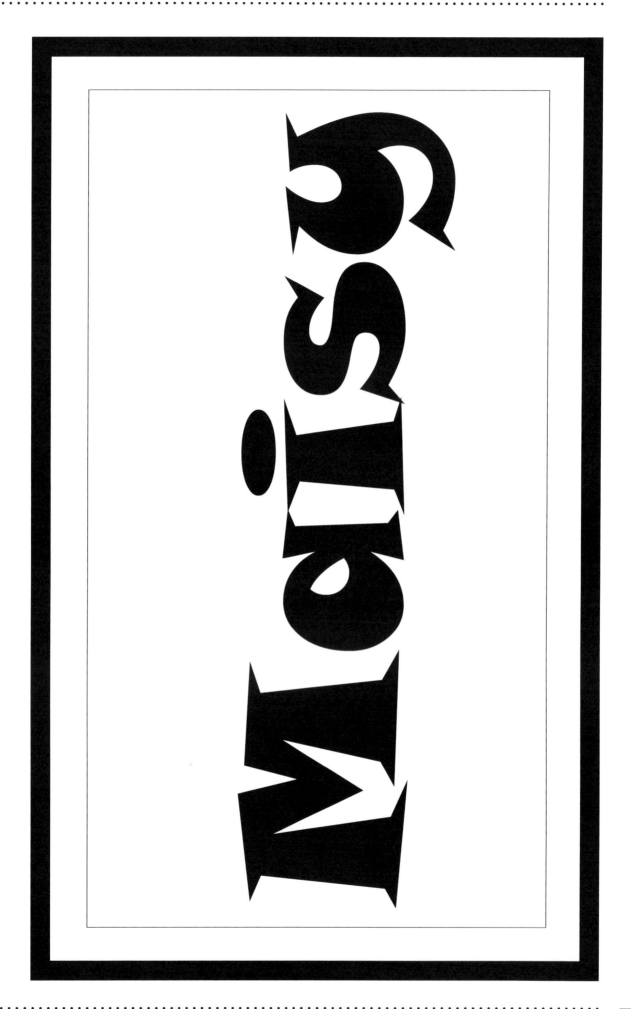

Selection and training

"Maisy's day"

The alarm went off and Maisy leapt out of bed. She needed to get a shower and wash her hair, as she was going to audition for the school play. She got her things ready, but her big sister was in the shower. She yelled for her to hurry up, telling her she needed to shower. Her mum called up the stairs, telling her to be quiet. "You are always so loud, Maisy," she said. "Leave your sister to shower."

Maisy tried to explain to her mum why it was so important.

"If it was that important, you should have told your sister last night," her mum replied. "Really, you are so disorganised."

Maisy gathered up all her stuff but couldn't find her school bag. She called down to her mum to see if she had seen it, but her mum just told her to look for it where she had last left it. "Honestly, Maisy, you really are forgetful," she said.

Finally her sister was out of the shower. Maisy quickly dashed in and slammed the door. She frantically got showered and washed her hair and then dashed back to her bedroom to dry her hair. Her mum came into her bedroom and threw her towel at her. "Maisy, you are so untidy," her mum said. "Please clean up after yourself. I'm fed up with doing it."

Maisy quickly hung up her towel and then dashed downstairs for breakfast. Her little brother was struggling with the milk container lid. Maisy gave him a tickle and then helped him. He giggled and smiled at her. "I love you, Maisy," he said as he gave her a cuddle.

Maisy's mum looked up and smiled at her. "You know you really are good with your brother," she said. "Thank you."

Maisy then grabbed all her things and dashed to the car. Her dad was waiting to take her to school. She leapt in and slammed the door, and her dad frowned; he was not happy. "Maisy, I wish you would treat things with more respect. You really seem to have no idea about how to look after things," he said.

Maisy apologised and then sorted out her homework. Her dad smiled. "You know, when your mum and I went to parents evening, your maths teacher was really pleased with your progress. He said you had really been working hard and that you were really focussed in his class. Shame the science teacher didn't think so. He said you often forgot your homework and were always talking to your friends. He said you were a really disruptive student. I can't understand how you can be so different."

"I know, Dad. I just really like the maths teacher. He really helps me."

Maisy and her dad finally got to school. "Is it auditions day today?" asked her dad.

Selection and training

"Yes," said Maisy.

"I hope it goes well. You deserve it. You have worked really hard on learning your lines. You really do have a great memory, and I know I am your dad, but I also think you have a lot of talent."

"Thanks, Dad. Fingers crossed."

Maisy jumped out of the car and went into the school. As she walked in through the doors her friends came to meet her, and they all walked to their form room together. As they entered Mr Smith, the deputy head, came in. He handed out the timetables for the auditions. Maisy was so excited to get one that she forgot to say "thank you" when he handed her the sheet.

"You know, Maisy Turner, you really are one of the rudest students I know. Not only don't you say please and thank you, but I also saw you teasing one of the year 7 the other day. I've got my eye on you, so I suggest that you sort yourself out."

"Yes, sir," answered Maisy.

"What was all that about?" asked her friend.

"I'm not sure. He seems to have it in for me. He's rather full of himself."

Maisy grabbed the timetable and then set off for maths, which was her first lesson. Mr Brown met her at the door. "How's my grade A student doing? Did you manage the homework?"

Maisy nodded and smiled. "Yes, sir, I did. Once I got going it was fine."

"Well done, Maisy. I really do think you have a brain for maths. You will go far."

"Thanks, sir."

Maisy finished maths and then went off for the audition. She was really nervous and didn't see Mr Smith walk around the corner. She bumped into him and knocked his books flying. "Oh, God. I am really sorry, sir. I wasn't concentrating. I was trying to . . ."

"I don't want to hear your excuses, young lady. You need to look where you're going. I am putting you in a lunchtime detention for running in the corridors. Perhaps that way you will learn that you are not the only person in this school."

Maisy started to argue but then drew a deep breath and remembered the audition. Instead she smiled and said, "Yes, sir," before turning and escaping into the drama room.

Selection and training

Labels

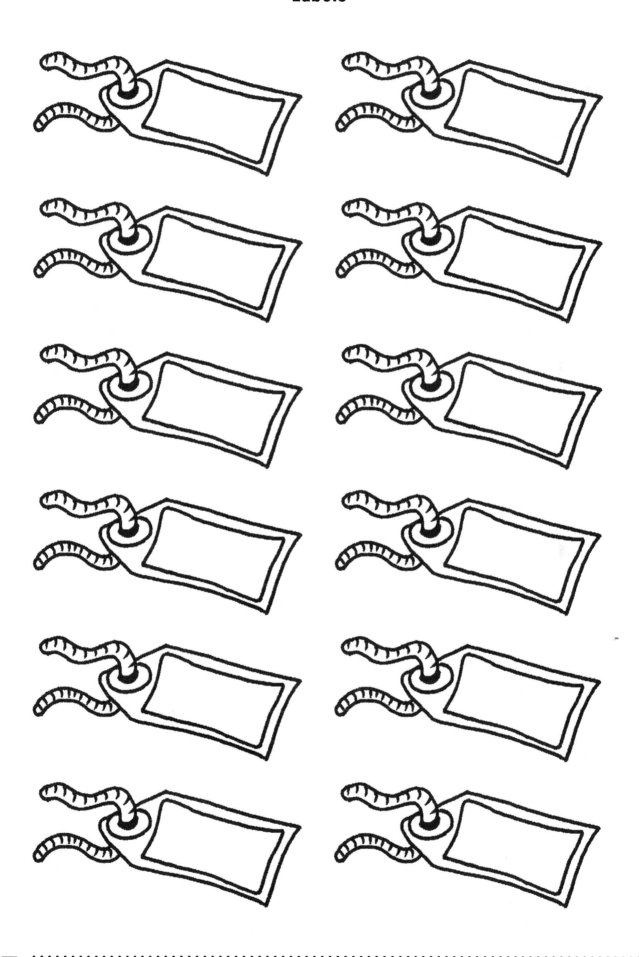

Selection and training

Training part 2: self-limiting beliefs part 2 (P/S)

Time of activity: 45 minutes

Objective

To develop a greater understanding about how our beliefs about ourselves impact on what we do and what we think we can do

Resources

Picture of the elephant and baby

Fleas in a jar

Elephant story

Flea in a glass jar experiment video clip (www.youtube.com/watch?v=TK2Hd9aO5HM)

Beliefs triangle poster

Activity

1. Discuss our beliefs and self-esteem and how they can change depending on what we are doing. If we think we are good at maths, we probably will be. If we have maths in the morning, our self-esteem will be high. If we don't think we are very good at art and we have art in the afternoon, our self-esteem will be lower.
2. Share the beliefs triangle poster.
3. Put up the "A mind stretched to a new idea never returns to its original dimension" quote and tell the elephant story.
4. Watch the flea in a glass jar video clip.
5. Discuss.
6. Ask the young people to work in pairs and create a poster to show the belief systems triangle.

Agree to the success criteria. These may include the following:

- Must show the link between beliefs, experiences and behaviour
- That we have a choice about how we think about things
- Must be eye catching so that people stop and look
- Must be easy to read
- Must get the message across that we have choices about what we believe about ourselves

7. Display all the posters around the room and ask the CYP to walk around in a silent viewing.
8. Join together and discuss what the posters have made them come up with. Why do they like them? What have they made them think about?
9. Explore why an understanding of self-limiting beliefs might be a useful piece of knowledge and understanding for the WBC.
10. Finish with a relaxation exercise before the CYP return to class.

Training part 2: basic skills

Copyright material from Alison Waterhouse (2021), *Wellbeing Champions*, Routledge

Selection and training

Selection and training

The elephant

What we believe about ourselves and the world actually creates the world we live in even if the belief is totally false.

Did you know that you can take a 2-tonne elephant, put a thin rope around its ankle and attach it to a small wooden peg in the ground and the elephant will not move?

The elephant could of course pull the stake out of the ground in an instant and go off wherever it wanted to and have a wonderful time. So why doesn't it?

When it was a baby elephant, a heavy chain was attached to its ankle and it was tied to a strong post in the ground. It learnt that every time it tried to get away it couldn't and if it kept trying it hurt its ankle. Consequently, it grew up with the belief "If you put a tie around my ankle, I cannot move" – a totally false belief in this instance. In fact, elephants have been known to die in fires tethered in this fashion because they believed they could not move.

Fleas have been shown to do a similar thing. A flea can jump 18 cm upwards from a table, which, given the fact that it is only 2.5 mm long, is quite amazing. It would be the same as us jumping over a 30-storey building. However, if a flea is kept in a sealed jar, it learns to avoid hitting its head by jumping only the height of the jar. If you then take the lid off the jar the flea will still jump only to the height it has learnt is safe, which means it doesn't escape.

This is exactly what your *beliefs* are like – both the good ones and the not so helpful ones. They are like a rope around your ankle, keeping you from doing things in your life.

Selection and training

The Beliefs System Triangle

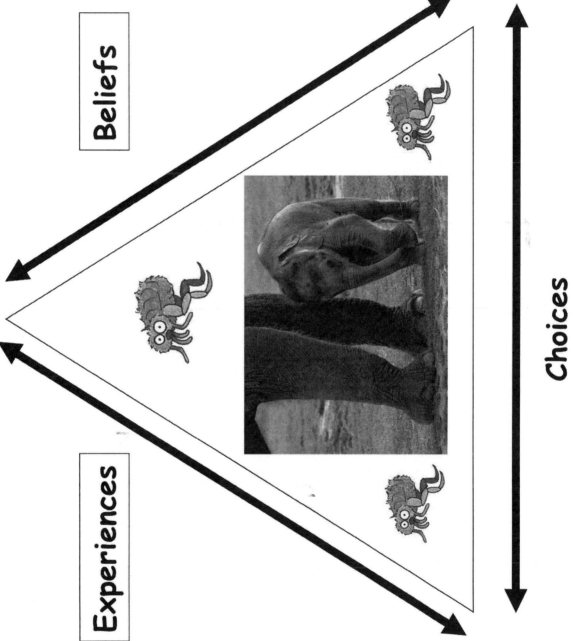

Selection and training

Training part 2: negativity bias (P/S)

Time of activity: 45 minutes

Objective

To understand why our brain notices and remembers negative things more quickly and powerfully than positive things and why challenging this has a positive impact on our wellbeing

Resources

Beat the Negativity Bias sheet
Beat the negativity bias
Shoeboxes
Pens, paper and glue
Magazines

The negativity bias and how to beat it video clip (www.youtube.com/watch?v=0LfteZ9k8YU&t=51s)

Activity

1. Watch the negativity bias video with the children and then discuss what they have learnt and what they think.
2. Stop the video clip before it starts to discuss how to beat the negativity bias and the brain's need to notice and think about all the negative things. Is this something the children recognise? Can they share an example of a time they couldn't get a negative event or incident out of their mind?
3. Share the next part of the video clip.
4. Discuss the 4 strategies:

   Awareness that the brain works in this way and why

   Looking for the positive or "Velcroing" the positive times

   Using gratitude to help us focus on the good things and stop the brain from searching for the negative things

5. Share the Beat the Negative Bias sheet with the children and ask them to work in small groups to fill this out and create a poster/postcard to remind them about letting the negative things slide off and sticking the good things in their mind.
6. Share the different posters or worksheet the children have come up with.
7. Ask the children to bring in a small box – a shoebox is ideal. Let them decorate this and make a box to collect "wow" moments in. This might be certificates, photos, reports, badges from guides or scouts, great pieces of work, etc.
8. Finish with a relaxation exercise to support the children in returning to a busy classroom.

Using a kudos folder – a box or folder that contains the good things we have done or achieved to remind us of the positive things in our life

Information:

The amygdala uses two thirds of its neurons to look for bad news or dangers. Once it detects them it fires the alarm, and those negative events and experiences then get quickly stored in our memory as a reference for future events. Positive memories are not stored as quickly.

Training part 2: basic skills

Selection and training

Selection and training

Training part 2: the bystander effect (P/S)

Time of activity: 45 minutes

Objective

To understand the bystander effect and ways to challenge this

Resources

The bystander effect: the science of empathy video clip (www.youtube.com/watch?v=Wy6eUTLzcU4)

The bystander effect video clip (www.youtube.com/watch?v=OSsPfbupCac)

The Bystander Effect Terminology sheet and Impact of Harmdoing sheet

Activity

1. Watch the bystander effect: the science of empathy and bystander effect video clips.
2. Ask the children to work in pairs and discuss what they have seen. What did they think? Have they ever been in a position where they wanted to help but didn't feel able to? Have they ever been in a position where they needed help?
3. While working in pairs, ask them to come up with multiple ways that people can harm others – bullying, harassment, violence, intimidation, unkindness, persecution, making fun of them, etc.
4. Share the different situations they have come up with and record them on the board.
5. Ask the pairs to think of the potential consequences for the targets of harmdoing. This could be fear, unhappiness, depression, suicide, lack of belief in themselves, etc.
6. Share the definition sheet with the children so that all can be clear about the terminology that will be used in the session.
7. Divide the children into 4 groups: targets, harmdoers, bystanders, school culture.
8. Ask them to work in their groups to answer the following questions:
   How is this person feeling whilst harm is going on?
   What happens as a result of the incident now or later?
   What lesson is being learnt from the incident of harmdoing?
9. Share the different points of view and impact the harmdoing can have on the different people involved.
10. Ask the children to work individually to record a time when they did something that harmed another person and the impact this had on the other person and themselves. The Impact of Harmdoing sheet can be used. Ask them to choose only something they are willing to share with the group.
11. Pose the question, What stops us from taking action? Discuss thoughts, ideas and information from the two video clips. Ask the children to work in pairs and then ask them to join with another pair and share their ideas.
12. Ask the class to identify the 5 different categories as they go, if possible.
13. Ask the children to work in pairs again and come up with an example for each of the areas.

Masks:

You watch a young person push another young person into a fence, and you walk away, pretending not to notice or see what they have done. You may even look away or in the opposite direction.

Training part 2: basic skills

200

Copyright material from Alison Waterhouse (2021), *Wellbeing Champions*, Routledge

Selection and training

Impact on them the target	
Impact on you the harmdoer	**The incident**

The impact of harmdoing on the harmdoer and the target

THE BYSTANDER EFFECT TERMINOLOGY

What is a bystander?

A bystander is a witness, someone who is in a position to know what is happening and is in a position to take action.

What is a passive bystander?

For some people, the word "bystander" means "passive." However, "bystander" is a neutral term. Therefore, a bystander can be passive or can become active. The following may be true of passivity in a bystander:

1. It may show itself as acceptance or approval of what the harmdoer is doing.

2. The bystander might not accept or approve, but by being passive others might think the bystander accepts or approves of the harmdoer's actions.

3. The harmdoer might think that their actions are accepted or approved of. This is likely to lead to further harmful actions.

4. Passivity can create a negative change in what the larger community sees as normal or acceptable behaviour.

5. The target and bystanders may begin to feel less trusting of others in general.

6. The passive bystander may feel guilt for not doing the right thing.

7. A very few witnesses might enjoy the suffering of another.

Complicity

Sometimes bystanders are not only passive but also complicit. The word "complicity" refers to any words, actions, or non-verbal reactions by which a bystander supports a harmdoer. This would include facial expressions and gestures, such as clapping or cheering, laughing, joining in with comments or actions or saying things to support the harmdoer. Sometimes bystanders may laugh because they are nervous and do not know what to do. This laughter can be interpreted by the harmdoer as supporting what they are doing and might even egg them on.

Moral courage

Moral courage is the ability and willingness to act according to our values (to do the right thing) even though others might disapprove of our actions or harm us. Moral courage means doing what you believe is the right thing even when these actions are different from the values, beliefs or expectations of other people.

Selection and training

Harmdoing

There is a lot of harmdoing (bullying, harassment, violence, intimidation) in schools, the community and the world both among young people and the adult population. Unfortunately, most young people experience being a target at some point, and at some point nearly everyone hurts another person through something they say or do, sometimes without even meaning to. Sadly, some young people become targets or regular harmdoers for long periods of time. This means that every young person is likely to experience being a bystander at some point.

Targets

Targets are the focus of the harmdoing – the target of the attack either physically or verbally or emotionally. They can experience distress, unhappiness and depression and have negative moods, all of which are the result of the actions of the harmdoers. The presence of passive bystanders makes targets feel worse, as they are aware that no one has stepped forward to help them. This raises the question, Why? Are they not worth it? Is something wrong with them? Studies show that people who are targets when bystanders are passive feel worse than if there are no witnesses.

Harmdoers

Harmdoers are the people who inflict harm on another person. Often the only way they can make what they have done acceptable to themselves is to devalue those they harm. This may mean focussing on their targets as outsiders, different, bad, strange, stupid, "them" not "us." For some people who are aggressive harmdoers, violent behaviour can become a habit. When harmdoers get what they want through their harmdoing behaviour, it reinforces this way of behaving.

INHIBITING BEHAVIOURS

Masks: pluralistic ignorance

The definition of masking behaviour is when people mask or cover their feelings. In other words, when they look at each other they do not show that anything is needed. In public, many people do not show they are upset; they wear a mask to cover their feelings. If you ask people they will say they are "fine." Their faces don't show feelings of fear, concern, anxiety, distress, anger, sadness, etc. Bystanders look around them, and all they see are other bystanders with no expressions on their faces and no clue as to what is needed, so no one does anything; they just walk by.

People tend to look to other people to see what they are doing or thinking before they act. If all the people around are wearing masks, all the bystanders decide there cannot be a problem and therefore they do not need to do anything.

Who, me? Diffusion of responsibility

When there are other people present, each person or bystander feels they have less responsibility because there are others present who could also respond. People look to each other to do something, which therefore means no one acts. Studies show that the more people there are at an emergency, the less likely it is that any one person helps.

Confusion: unclear as to whether help is needed

When the bystanders who are around and watching are unclear if help is needed, they are less likely to help. People receive more help if they call for help. However, targets don't always want to be seen as needing help, as being a target can feel shameful. This means that the targets choose to act as if there is nothing wrong and everything is okay. Sometimes they can even laugh or joke. When they do this it is really hard for bystanders to understand if help is really needed.

Danger: danger or cost of helping

Sometimes bystanders understand that by helping they could put themselves in danger, either at the time or later. Sometimes the emotional cost and effort of helping the target can be seen as being too high. If the target is unpopular, then by helping them the active bystander could be picked on, teased or even excluded from a group. If the target is someone the active bystander does not like, the target might turn to the bystander for continued support and friendship after the event, and this may be something they do not want. Individuals often don't like people because their group dislikes them. When this is the case the underling belief is that there is something wrong with the individual because they are not liked.

Fear: fear of disapproval

Fear of disapproval refers to looking foolish or getting something wrong whilst others are watching. The bystander may be unsure as to whether they have the skills to help or if they can solve the problem or make a difference. This may be linked to the judgement of others. When a person chooses to act or do something in front of a group they are likely to feel a little self-conscious and anxious. In addition, if they are acting contrary to the opinion or attitudes of an individual or group, they are likely to feel very uncomfortable.

Selection and training

Training part: resilience (P/S)

Objective
To discuss and identify what enables people to keep going when life gets difficult

Resources
Book list
Book tasting information sheet

Things That Keep Us Going When Life Gets Tough sheet

Activity

1. Set up a book tasting session with the children (see information sheet for how to do this).
2. Set out a variety of books on each table so that the children are able to access different books.
3. Challenge the children to identify as many things as possible that support the different characters in continuing on when life gets difficult.
4. Remind the children that this is a book tasting – they do not need to read the whole thing. By tasting the different books they can choose which one they wish to read in full later.
5. Once the children have read their books they can fill out the Things That Keep Us Going When Life Gets Tough sheet for the different characters.
6. Once the children have read several of the books and you have collected the information, share what they have found and discuss the different strategies the characters have used.
7. Discuss with the CYP which strategies they have used. Which ones do they fancy trying in the future?
8. Finish with a calming relaxation exercise to help the CYP return to the busy classroom or school.

Time of activity: 45 minutes

Training part 2: basic skills

Copyright material from Alison Waterhouse (2021), *Wellbeing Champions*, Routledge

Selection and training

BOOKS TO USE FOR THE BOOK TASTING ON RESILIENCE

1. *Pete the Cat and His Four Groovy Buttons* by Eric Litwin
2. *Jabari Jumps* by Gaia Cornwall
3. *The Tiny Seed* by Eric Carle
4. *A Perfectly Messed-Up Story* by Patrick McDonnell
5. *The Adventures of Beekle: The Unimaginary Friend* by Dan Santat
6. *Strictly No Elephants* by Lisa Mantchev
7. *A Mouse So Small* by Angela McAllister
8. *The Harmonica* by Tony Johnston
9. *Rose Blanche* by Ian McEwan
10. *Emmanuel's Dream: The True Story Of Emmanuel Ofosu Yeboah* by Laurie Thompson
11. *The Hugging Tree* by Jill Neimark
12. *Salt in His Shoes: Michael Jordan* by Deloris Jordan
13. *The Boy Who Harnessed the Wind* by William Kamkwamba, *et al.*
14. *El Deafo* by Cece Bell
15. *The Thing Lou Couldn't Do* by Ashley Spires
16. *Out of My Mind* by Sharon M. Draper
17. *Ben's Trumpet* by Rachel Isadora
18. *Hope in a Ballet Shoe* by Michaela DePrince
19. *Hatchet* by Gary Paulsen

Resource

1. A box of puppets or a range of finger puppets.

Selection and training

Things that help us keep going when life gets tough

Internal strategies or characteristics

External support

Character

The challenge they are facing.

Selection and training

BOOK TASTING INFORMATION

1. Set up your classroom as a restaurant and put a big menu board up to tell the children about the book tasting.

2. Each table needs to be set out with a tablecloth (checkered ones are good and have a brilliant effect), a candle (you can get battery-operated ones), napkins and plates.

3. Put a book menu on each plate.

4. Put a variety of books linked to resilience (choose depending on the age group and the children you have in the class) on each table. Ensure that you are mindful of the children and their backgrounds and their ability to read. Ensure you have a selection of books for different reading ages, some with no words.

5. Ask the children to sit at a table and choose a starter book to "taste." They have 3 minutes to look at the book, read the blurb, look at the cover and read the first few pages.

6. After 3 minutes you will ring the bell. Then they need to write up the Things That Keep Us Going When Life Gets Tough sheet for one of the characters in the book they tasted.

7. After the short write-up, explain that they can now choose their main course, and they can have 5 minutes looking at and tasting this book. Then you will ring the bell and they can write up the Things That Keep Us Going When Life Gets Tough sheet for this book.

8. Their penultimate choice is their pudding or dessert course. They will be given 3 minutes to explore and taste their dessert book. Then you will ring the bell and they will be able to write up the Things That Keep Us Going When Life Gets Tough sheet for that book.

9. Their final choice is their coffee and mints course. For this they will have 2 minutes to choose and taste their book.

10. When the tasting is over discuss the books and then move the children into groups so that they can continue reading their first or second favourite book.

Selection and training

On your table you have

Tasting Etiquette

1. Choose one book to "taste."
You don't need to eat/read the entire thing to know if you like it Try a little bite!

2. Critique your selection by filling in answers on your menu.

3. Repeat steps 1-2 for another dish/book.

4. Enjoy!

Menu

Selection and training

Training part 2: confidentiality (P/S)

Time of activity: 45 minutes

Objective

To enable CYP to understand what confidentiality is
To help the WBC understand why confidentiality is so important in the work they will engage in

Resources

Paper
Pens, pencils

Activity

1. Act out a short scene where a young person tells you about something they are interested in and an activity they have been engaged in related to this. Example: a young person tells you how much they love horseback riding/skating/mountain biking and how they have been to a special event at the weekend.
2. Now act out a short scene where a young person tells you about a row they had with their friend and how the friend left them out and didn't invite them to their bowling party.
3. Ask the children whether they think you should repeat the information you have been given to another young person. If not, why not?
4. Introduce the word "confidentiality."
5. Ask the children to work in pairs and find/write a definition they feel shows what the word means.
6. Ask the CYP to work in small groups. Ask the following questions and explore what they think. Ask them to discuss them in their group and then to share.
   How do they think confidentiality will affect the work they do as WBC?
   Why will it be important?
   What would happen if people thought everything they said would be talked about?
   Should everything be confidential?
   Will there be times when information has to be shared?
   When information might have to be shared?
   Who should information be shared with?
   How could the WBC make sure that the children they support understand confidentiality?
7. Ask the groups to write an Important Information leaflet sharing what confidentiality is, why it is important, what to do if they are unsure about something as a Wellbeing Champion and a list of times when it will be important to "think before they talk."
8. Share the information sheets with each other and then choose one to adopt as the WBC policy on confidentiality.
9. Finish with a calming relaxation exercise to help the children return to the busy classroom or school.

Training part 2: basic skills

Selection and training

Training part 2: let's talk mental health (P)

Time of activity: 45 minutes

Objective

To explore mental health and clarify language around this

To have consistent and accessible language to talk about mental health and wellbeing

To understand the difference between everyday feelings and overwhelming feelings

Resources

Colour wheel

Colour spectrum chart

"Talking mental health" video clip (www.youtube.com/watch?v=nCrjevx3-Js&t=195s)

Activity

1. What do we mean when we talk about mental health?
2. Ask the CYP to share their thoughts and ideas. Discuss what they come up with.
3. Give the CYP the definition "Mental health is about our feelings, our thinking, our emotions and our moods – things you can't really see but that affect our lives in lots of ways."
4. Explore the difference between mental health and physical health. The main difference is that we can't always see it in the same way we can see a broken arm or chickenpox.
5. Show the video clip "Talking mental health."
6. Discuss what they noticed in the animation. Clarify "small, everyday feelings." Are there any other examples the class can give? Clarify that these feelings can change according to what is happening during our day.
7. Share the colour wheel with the children. Choose different colours to represent different feelings – e.g. red angry, blue sad. Now share the colour spectrum for one of the feelings. Help the children understand that darker colours represent stronger feelings. Example: light blue may be sad, whereas dark blue could be miserable or devastated.
8. Explore strategies the children use to cope with small, everyday feelings to make them more manageable. Example: if you feel fed up you might go and read your favourite book or comic to cheer yourself up.
9. Introduce the term "mental ill health." This is a broad term often used by us and others as an umbrella term that includes both mental illness and mental health problems.

Mental illness is a disorder diagnosed by a medical professional that significantly interferes with an individual's cognitive, emotional or social abilities. There are different types of mental illness, and they occur with varying degrees of severity. Examples include mood disorders (such as depression, anxiety and bipolar disorder), psychotic disorders (such as schizophrenia), eating disorders and personality disorders.

Mental health problems also interfere with a person's cognitive, emotional or social abilities but may not meet the criteria for a diagnosed mental illness. Mental health problems often occur as a result of life stressors and are usually less severe and of shorter duration than mental illnesses.

10. Ask the CYP why knowing about mental health might be useful when working as a WBC. Explore and discuss.
11. Finish with a relaxation exercise before the children return to class.

Training part 2: basic skills

Copyright material from Alison Waterhouse (2021), *Wellbeing Champions*, Routledge

Selection and training

Training part 2: let's talk mental health (S)

Time of activity: 45 minutes

Objective

To explore mental health and clarify language around this

To have consistent and accessible language to talk about mental health and wellbeing

To understand the difference between everyday feelings and overwhelming feelings

Resources

Colour wheel
Colour spectrum card
Venn diagram

"We all have mental health" video clip (www.youtube.com/watch?v=DxIDKZHW3-E)

Activity

1. Ask the children what they believe the term "mental health" means.
2. "Mental health is about our feelings, our thinking, our emotions and our moods. Looking after our mental health is just as important as looking after our physical health."
3. Set up two large pieces of paper, one labelled OK Language and one labelled Not OK Language.
4. Watch the "We all have mental health" video clip.
5. Discuss what was happening for Sasha and Andre in the video.
6. Explore with the CYP the differences between Sasha's and Andre's feelings. What sort of self-care strategies have they used in the past? What could they do if they become worried about someone?
7. Give the children the Venn diagram and ask them to complete it in groups. Small everyday feeling and emotions and overwhelming feelings and emotions.
8. Discuss what the CYP have identified and come up with.
9. Share the colour wheel and explain that it can represent different feelings – the red could be anger, the blue sadness. Then share the colour spectrum. If a colour represents a particular feeling, then the different shades represent different intensities of that feeling.
10. Introduce the term "mental ill health." This is a broad term often used by us and others as an umbrella term that includes both mental illness and mental health problems.

Mental illness is a disorder diagnosed by a medical professional that significantly interferes with an individual's cognitive, emotional or social abilities. There are different types of mental illness, and they occur with varying degrees of severity. Examples include mood disorders (such as depression, anxiety and bipolar disorder), psychotic disorders (such as schizophrenia), eating disorders and personality disorders.

Mental health problems also interfere with a person's cognitive, emotional or social abilities but may not meet the criteria for a diagnosed mental illness. Mental health problems often occur as a result of life stressors and are usually less severe and of shorter duration than mental illnesses.

11. Introduce the topic of language and refer back to the sheets you set up earlier – OK Language and Not OK Language. Ask the children to write on Post-it notes different words and then place them on the correct sheet.
12. Ask the CYP why knowing about mental health is useful for their new role as WBC.
13. Finish the session with a relaxation activity to support the CYP in transitioning back into school life.

Training part 2: basic skills

Selection and training

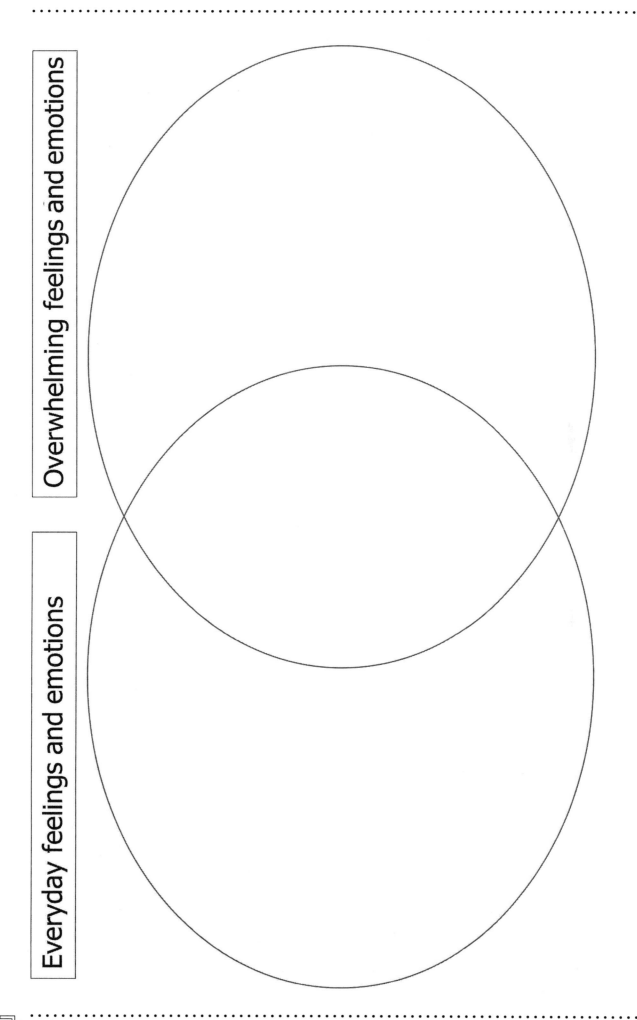

Selection and training

Training part 2: respect (P)

Objective
To be able to share what the word "respect" means and to give examples of what would be respectful and what would be disrespectful

Resources
Access to the internet
Paper and pens

Time of activity: 45 minutes

Activity

1. Write the word "respect" on the board and then ask the children to work in pairs to come up with:
   - A definition
   - A picture showing respect
   - A poem about respect or a song
   - A quote about respecting others
   - A quote about self-respect
2. Ask the children to lay their collection out on the table, and then ask the pairs to walk around and undertake a silent viewing.
3. Discuss what they have seen and what this has made them think about.
4. Ask the children to create a list showing disrespectful attitudes and behaviours and respectful attitudes and behaviour. They can do this in a variety of ways:
   - A series of pictures
   - A table
   - A mind map
   - A list
5. Share the different ways the children have used and the lists they have come up with.
6. After they have shared the different methods they have used as well as their lists, ask them to work in groups and discuss how they believe respect should be taught, both at home and in school.
7. Ask the children to share the different ways they have come up with. If they would like to run a session with a group of other CYP, this could be set up. They could also undertake an assembly about respect if this is appropriate.
8. Finish with a calming relaxation exercise to help the children return to the busy classroom or school.

Training part 2: basic skills

Selection and training

Training part 2: respect (S)

Time of activity: 45 minutes

Objective

To be able to share what the word "respect" means and to give examples of what would be respectful and what would be disrespectful

Resources

Respect cloud picture
Access to the computer

Activity

1. Share a "respect" word cloud with the children and discuss what it shows.
2. Ask them to work in pairs and define the words "respect" and "disrespect".
3. Working in pairs, ask them to create a montage for respect and disrespect.
4. This needs to be made up of words, pictures, quotes, sayings, songs, poems, etc.
5. When the children have finished create an exhibition to share their work.
6. Discuss what they have learnt from the task:
   What have they found out that is important to them?
   What have they learnt?
   How will this impact on their behaviour in the future?
   How will they challenge disrespectful behaviour in the future?
   How will they promote respectful behaviour?
   What one thing could the WBC do that would promote respectful behaviour?
7. Finish with a relaxation exercise to support the CYP in returning to a busy classroom.

Training part 2: basic skills

Copyright material from Alison Waterhouse (2021), *Wellbeing Champions*, Routledge

Selection and training

Training part 1: be your own life coach (P/S)

Time of activity: 2 × 45 minutes

Objective
To develop the skills to be your own life coach

Resources
Pictures of coaches working with people

Speech bubble Post-it notes

Gold coins

Activity

1. Divide the class into groups. Ask each group to look at the coaching pictures and identify what skills the coaches need to have to help/support/develop/strengthen their teams/players.
2. Imagine that the coaches' comments are like gold coins being put in the bank and that the players' negative comments/thoughts make the gold coins vanish. For the teams/players to be successful the bank balance needs to be healthy.
3. Choose one of the pictures and then in groups write on the gold coins some of the comments the coach might use to build their team/players up and make them feel positive about themselves and their abilities.
4. Share some of these comments with the other groups. What is important to include in the comments? It is important for the person being coached to be able to trust their coach, so the comments have to be honest, contain examples and motivate them.
5. Choose the top 10 comments.
6. Remind the children and young people about being their own life coach. Help them explore the self-talk they use when doing a task or piece of work.
7. Give the children Post-it note speech bubbles and ask them to write some of their positive self-talk and some of their not so positive self-talk.
8. Ask the CYP to share what they have come up with. Explore the language they have used and highlight the positive. Ask the question, How will you know what sort of self-talk someone is using when you listen to them? Discuss how people talk about themselves when they engage in conversation.
9. Ask the CYP to work in pairs and give an example of someone talking where there is a lot of negative self-talk going on in their head. Share some of the sketches.
10. Ask the CYP to think about how it feels when they see people struggling. What do they want to do?
11. Ask the children to think what happens if a parent or teacher does a task for us each time we get stuck. Introduce the phrase "they are stealing our learning opportunity." Think about what this means. How can we help if doing the task or thing is not supportive?

Introduce the concept of scaffolding learning – being there to support but not steal the opportunity.

Training part 1: designing and co-producing

216

Copyright material from Alison Waterhouse (2021), *Wellbeing Champions*, Routledge

Selection and training

Training part 1: designing and co-producing

Training part 1: be your own life coach (P)

Time of activity: 2 × 45 minutes

Objective
To develop the skills to be your own life coach

Resources
Pictures of coaches working with people

Speech bubble Post-it notes
Gold coins

Activity

1. Divide the class into groups. Ask each group to look at the coaching pictures and identify what skills the coaches need to have to help/support/develop/strengthen their teams/players.
2. Imagine that the coaches' comments are like gold coins being put in the bank and that the players' negative comments/thoughts make the gold coins vanish. For the teams/players to be successful the bank balance needs to be healthy.
3. Choose one of the pictures and then in groups write on the gold coins some of the comments the coach might use to build their team/players up and make them feel positive about themselves and their abilities.
4. Share some of these comments with the other groups. What is important to include in the comments? It is important for the person being coached to be able to trust their coach, so the comments have to be honest, contain examples and motivate them.
5. Choose the top 10 comments.
6. Remind the children and young people about being their own life coach. Help them explore the self-talk they use when doing a task or piece of work.
7. Give the children Post-it note speech bubbles and ask them to write some of their positive self-talk and some of their not so positive self-talk.
8. Ask the CYP to share what they have come up with. Explore the language they have used and highlight the positive. Ask the question, How will you know what sort of self-talk someone is using when you listen to them? Discuss how people talk about themselves when they engage in conversation.
9. Ask the CYP to work in pairs and give an example of someone talking where there is a lot of negative self-talk going on in their head. Share some of the sketches.
10. Ask the CYP to think about how it feels when they see people struggling. What do they want to do?
11. Ask the children to think what happens if a parent or teacher does a task for us each time we get stuck. Introduce the phrase "they are stealing our learning opportunity." Think about what this means. How can we help if doing the task or thing is not supportive?

Introduce the concept of scaffolding learning – being there to support but not steal the opportunity.

Copyright material from Alison Waterhouse (2021), *Wellbeing Champions*, Routledge

217

Selection and training

Training part 1: be your own life coach (S)

Time of activity: 2 × 45 minutes

Objective
To develop the skills to be your own life coach

Resources
Pictures of coaches working with people

Speech bubble Post-it notes
Gold coins

Activity

1. Divide the class into groups. Ask each group to look at the coaching pictures and identify what skills the coaches need to have to help/support/develop/strengthen their teams/players.
2. Imagine that the coaches' comments are like gold coins being put in the bank and that the players' negative comments/thoughts make the gold coins vanish. For the teams/players to be successful the bank balance needs to be healthy.
3. Choose one of the pictures and then in groups write on the gold coins some of the comments the coach might use to build their team/players up and make them feel positive about themselves and their abilities.
4. Share some of these comments with the other groups. What is important to include in the comments? It is important for the person being coached to be able to trust their coach, so the comments have to be honest, contain examples and motivate them.
5. Choose the top 10 comments.
6. Remind the children and young people about being their own life coach. Help them explore the self-talk they use when doing a task or piece of work.
7. Give the children Post-it note speech bubbles and ask them to write some of their positive self-talk and some of their not so positive self-talk.
8. Ask the CYP to share what they have come up with. Explore the language they have used and highlight the positive. Ask the question, How will you know what sort of self-talk someone is using when you listen to them? Discuss how people talk about themselves when they engage in conversation.
9. Ask the CYP to work in pairs and give an example of someone talking where there is a lot of negative self-talk going on in their head. Share some of the sketches.
10. Ask the CYP to think about how it feels when they see people struggling. What do they want to do?
11. Ask the children to think what happens if a parent or teacher does a task for us each time we get stuck. Introduce the phrase "they are stealing our learning opportunity." Think about what this means. How can we help if doing the task or thing is not supportive?

Introduce the concept of scaffolding learning – being there to support but not steal the opportunity.

Training part 1: designing and co-producing

Copyright material from Alison Waterhouse (2021), *Wellbeing Champions*, Routledge

Selection and training

Selection and training

Training part 2: neurodiversity (P/S)

Time of activity: 45 minutes

Objective

To understand that every brain is unique

To be able to define what "neurotypical" and "neurodiverse" mean and give examples

Resources

You're so Clumsy Charley by Jane Binnion

I Have Bees in My Brain by Trish Hammond

The Higgledy-Piggledy Pigeon by Don Winn

Neurodiversity poster

Pens, paper and art materials

Activity

1. Share the What is Neurodiversity? poster with the children.
2. Discuss and share thoughts and feelings.
3. What questions does it make them want to ask?
4. What thoughts do they have about different brains?
5. Ask the children to work in pairs and create a poster for their classroom about the benefits of being in a neurodiverse classroom.
6. Share the posters as they are being created and get feedback from the other children. Remember the feedback sandwich: I like . . . It would be good if you could expand or clarify . . . I think my favourite bit is . . . Because
7. When completed hold an exhibition to share the work and get feedback from other CYP for the WBC.
8. Read the books *You're so Clumsy Charley*, *I Have Bees in My Brain* and *The Higgledy-Piggledy Pigeon*. For older children try *The Goldfish Boy* by Lisa Thompson, *Being Miss Nobody* by Tamsin Winter or *The Boy with the Butterfly Mind* by Victoria Williamson.
9. Discuss why they think that understanding neurodiversity is important for WBC and how it may help them with the work they will do.
10. Finish with a relaxation exercise to support the CYP in returning to the busy school environment.

Note: For older children you could ask them to identify a list of neurodiverse brains and 3 things each brain is often good at. This can include dyslexic brains, dyspraxic brains, ASD brains and OCD brains.

Training part 2: basic skills

Selection and training

What is neurodiversity?

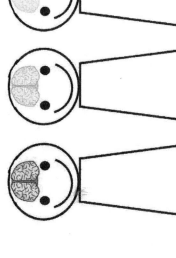

This is Sam

This is Sam's brain

These are Sam's friends. They all have brains too. No two brains are the same. This is NEURODIVERSITY. All brains are different and unique.

Sam and friends are happy with their individual differences. They support each other and value the strengths that they each bring to their group.

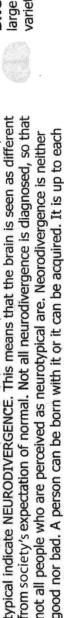

Neuro – relating to nerves or the nervous system

Diverse – showing a large amount of variety; very different

Some people's brains are similar and so they are labelled the same. Some of these labels are: typical, autistic, dyslexic, dyspraxic, bipolar. All of these labels except typical indicate NEURODIVERGENCE. This means that the brain is seen as different from society's expectation of normal. Not all neurodivergence is diagnosed, so that not all people who are perceived as neurotypical are. Neurodivergence is neither good nor bad. A person can be born with it or it can be acquired. It is up to each neurodiverse person to decide what support they would like.

Selection and training

Training part 2: conflict resolution part 1 (P/S)

Time of activity: 45 minutes

Objective
To enable CYP to use the restorative justice process to support others in managing a conflict and finding a way forward

Resources
Restorative script	Method descriptions
"Restorative" definition	Scenarios
"Retributive" definition	

Activity

1. Divide the CYP into groups and give each group a scenario to discuss. They have to decide if the scenario is a "green" or a "red" scenario. Red represents "retributive," from the retributive theory of justice that considers punishment, if proportionate, to be the best response to crime. Green represents "restorative" and reflects the restorative approach to justice, which focusses on the needs of victims, offenders and the involved community instead of just punishment for the offender.
2. Ask the CYP to share their scenarios and which colour they think they are.
3. If the CYP think the scenario is a red, or retributive, scenario, they can be asked to identify the method used to manage it: stealing the conflict, sticky plaster, taking away and reducing the responsibility, focussing on broken rules (see definition sheet).
4. Look at each scenario and identify the key points.
5. The trainer should then act out 2 scenarios:
   (Ask the CYP to observe carefully, as they will need to ask questions.)

   Scenario 1: At playtime a group did not let a child join in a game and the child kicked out. The child has been sent to the teacher.

   Scenario 2: A senior member of staff walks down the corridor to find a child has been sent out of the room for throwing something at another child who was teasing them about not being able to do the work.

   In the first demonstration, the trainer re-enacts the scenario from a restorative point of view using the following:

   I can see you are . . . (angry, sad, upset).
   What has happened?
   What were you thinking at the time?
   How were you feeling at the time?
   Who else was affected?
   What can we do to put things right?

6. Discuss the differences.
7. Ask the CYP to act out one of the scenarios both ways.
8. Finish with a calming relaxation exercise to help the CYP return to the busy classroom or school.

Training part 2: basic skills

Selection and training

METHOD DESCRIPTIONS

Steal the conflict

Stealing the conflict occurs when adults intervene and tell people off. They do not stop and ask people about what happened or how they felt or how they would like the situation to be rectified. This means that the CYP haven't been involved in the decision or felt listened to in any way.

Selection and training

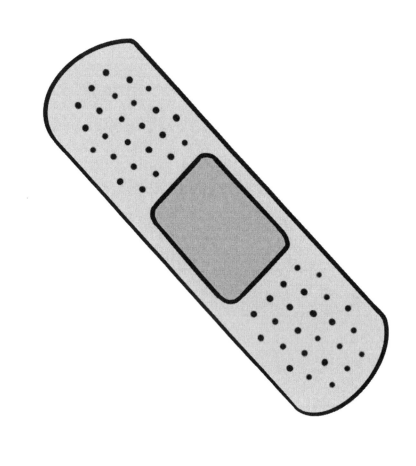

Use sticky plasters

Using sticky plasters occurs when the conflict hasn't been talked about or resolved, but the children involved have been told to go and get on. As with a wound that hasn't been cleaned, the damage can often fester and erupt into a big situation later.

Selection and training

This occurs when adults think only about the rules that have been broken and not how people felt or even why the situation may have happened. They do not help the CYP work out how to repair the relationship.

Only think about broken rules

Selection and training

Reduce responsibility

Reduced responsibility occurs when adults decide what has happened and why and then punish those involved. They do not involve the CYP in exploring why the situation happened, how each of them felt and why they behaved as they did. They don't support the CYP in listening to each other or repairing the relationship. Punishment is the focus, with the belief that if you punish people they will not commit the crime again.

Restorative justice is an approach to justice that focuses on the needs of the victims and the offenders, as well as the involved community, instead of just punishing the offender. Victims take an active role in the process, while offenders are encouraged to take responsibility for their actions, "to repair the harm they've done—by apologizing, returning stolen money, or community service". It provides help for the offender in order to avoid future offences. Restorative justice that fosters dialogue between victim and offender shows the highest rates of victim satisfaction and offender accountability.

Selection and training

Retributive justice is a theory of justice that considers punishment, if proportionate, to be the best response to crime. When an offender breaks the law, s/he thereby forfeits or suspends her/his right to something of equal value.

"Let the punishment fit the crime" is a principle that means the severity of penalty for a misdeed or wrongdoing should be reasonable and proportionate to the severity of the crime. The concept is common to most cultures throughout the world. However, the judgment of whether a punishment is appropriately severe can vary greatly between cultures and individuals.

Selection and training

Scenario 1
Tom and Ben were on the playground at lunchtime. Mrs Stockton was on lunch duty. When she looked across the playground she saw them arguing with each other, and then they started to push each other. She shouted across the playground for the two boys to stop. The boys carried on. Mrs Stockton marched over and pulled the boys apart. She then insisted they follow her to see Mr Brown, who put them in detention for the rest of the week for fighting, which was against the school rules.
br

Scenario 2
Sally ran over to Mrs Bell with tears running down her face. Mrs Bell asked Sally what on earth had happened. Sally carried on sobbing but managed to say that Karen and Trisha had been calling her names. Mrs Bell was very cross. She sent for the two girls, proceeded to tell them off and then sent them to see Mr Greg, the head teacher. She then turned to Sally and said, "I don't know why you don't just stay away from them. You know they always upset you."
St.con

Scenario 3
Toby had been very upset for several days. When he came home from school he was quiet and just went to his room. His mum and dad were very worried about him. They tried to talk to him, but he just said that nothing was wrong. Finally he talked to his big brother and told him that some of the boys in the class above him were making him give them all his sweets at break time. Toby's mum and dad went into school, and the other boy was excluded for a week.
St.con

Scenario 4
Tabitha and Meg were arguing in the classroom. Mrs Ryan ignored them and continued to work with her group. The two girls continued, and the other children around them couldn't carry on with their work. Mrs Ryan now decided that enough was enough and got up and told them to stop. She said, "You are both in big trouble. I have watched your silly squabble stop all the other children on your table working." She asked Meg to go to one end of the classroom and Tabitha to the other.
Stpl

Scenario 5
Mrs Godfrey asked all the class to hand their homework in as they left her classroom. All the children handed in their folders as they walked past her table. John approached her and looked quite worried. "No homework, John?" asked Mrs Godfrey. "I'm sorry, Miss. I left it in my dad's car this morning," John said. "You know what the school rule is, John. Homework or detention, no excuses," Mrs Godfrey replied. John continued to argue with Mrs Godfrey, finally shouting at her and storming out of the class. Mrs Godfrey spoke to his class teacher, who put him in detention for being rude to the teacher. He had to copy out the school's golden rules, as he had broken them.
br

Scenario 6
Henry and Fred were working on their project together when Fred knocked over the paint pot and all the water went over the painting they had been working on. Henry became very cross and shouted at Fred for being careless. Fred became very upset and shouted back at Henry, telling him he was stupid. Henry then told Fred that the painting was useless, as he wasn't very good at painting and he'd never really wanted to work with him. Their class teacher intervened at that point and told them to stop arguing, as they had a lot of work to get done. He asked Fred to work outside the classroom and sent Henry to the wet area in the class to work.
Stpl

Selection and training

Scenario 7
Debbie and her sister Macey were playing in the garden with their new bikes. They had built a special obstacle course and were practising. Debbie wanted to make the course wider, but Macey didn't. Macey felt it was fine as it was. They started to argue and shout at each other. Hearing the commotion, their mum came out. The girls were both shouting and screaming at each other, being very rude. Their mum raised her voice and sent them both indoors to their room, saying that she would call them down later when they had time to cool off. When they came down, their mum said that she didn't want to hear any more about the argument.
Rr

Scenario 8
Alex and Paul were playing football at the playing fields with their team. Alex missed the goal and Paul shouted out that he was stupid. Alex heard him and called him a rude name. Paul didn't like this and ran after him. Their coach told them to stop and sent Paul back to the changing room and Alex to sit on the side of the pitch. When their parents came to pick them up, the coach talked to them about how they had behaved. He then said he was banning them from 2 matches and that when they came back he didn't want to hear any more about the argument.
rr

Scenario 9
David and Adam had been in the same class since September. They had been working on a new topic together and had created a really lovely topic book. Their class teacher, Mr Drew, had asked them to show the book at showing assembly on Friday. David had taken the book home Thursday night to finish off an important picture, and he had forgotten to bring it on Friday morning. Adam was really angry with him, and they had an argument. Adam was very cross with David and shouted and called him stupid. David got cross at being called stupid and pushed Adam, who then fell over. Mr Drew spent playtime with both the boys talking about what had happened. David then tried to phone his mum. She wasn't able to bring in the topic book, as she was working, but Mr Drew agreed that they could show their work the following week. Adam and David spent lunchtime together working on the project in the library.

Scenario 10
Joshua ran into school and raced towards his classroom. As he ran around the corner he flew into Mrs Jones, the new teacher. She dropped her books and bounced into the wall. Joshua just yelled at her to get out of the way. Mrs Jones was not happy and reported Joshua to the head teacher, telling him about the very rude young person she had met.

Mr Banks, the head teacher, asked Joshua and Mrs Jones to meet him in his office, where he asked them both what had happened. Mrs Jones explained that Joshua had been running carelessly in school and had barged into her, knocking her flying, and that he was obviously a very rude and dangerous young man. Mr Banks then asked Joshua what had happened, and he said that he had been running to the classroom to get Tim's asthma inhaler, and Mrs Jones had deliberately gotten in his way and nearly stopped him from getting the medicine.

Mr Banks then helped both Mrs Jones and Joshua apologise to each other and work out what to do in the future if Tim needed his inhaler.

Selection and training

Scenario 11	**Scenario 12**
Mrs Thomas was Stacey's mum. Stacey had lost her coat in school, and Mrs Thomas was very cross, as it had cost her a lot of money. Stacey had told her mum that she had hung it on her peg but now it was missing. Mrs Thomas went to see Stacey's teacher, Mrs Finn. Stacey's mum was very cross and shouted at Mrs Finn, telling her that it was her fault that Stacey had lost her coat. Mrs Thomas then stormed out of school. Mrs Hick, the head teacher, phoned Mrs Thomas and asked her to come to school to meet up with her the next day. When Mrs Thomas came into school Mrs Hick talked to her calmly about what had happened, and they were able to trace back where Stacey had put her coat – in the library. Mrs Hick asked Stacey's mum to make things right with Stacey's class teacher. Mrs Thomas was very embarrassed that she had been so rude and made such a fuss and so brought her a bunch of flowers and a card to apologise.	Tim had only been in Mr Gower's class for a week when Lisa found him taking a chocolate bar out of her lunchbox. She went and told Mr Gower what had happened. Mr Gower asked both of them to come into class at lunchtime so that they could talk about what Lisa had seen. At first Tim denied what had happened, saying that Lisa was a liar. Lisa got upset but insisted that he had taken it. Mr Gower made sure that they both had time to talk and say what they had seen, felt and done. Finally, Tim owned up and said he had stolen the bar. Lisa was able to tell him how horrible it felt knowing someone had touched her food or wondering if they had. Tim was able to say he was sorry for what he had done, and they both agreed that it would only be right if he did something to make up for what he had done. Tim would do double duty that week; his own lunchtime monitors role and also take Lisa's job for the week.

Selection and training

Training part 2: conflict resolution part 2 (P/S)

Time of activity: 45 minutes

Objective

To enable CYP to use the restorative justice process to support others in managing a conflict and finding a way forward

Resources

Restorative script
"Restorative" definition
"Retributive" definition

Method descriptions
Scenarios
Ground rules

Activity

1. Ask the CYP to act out a scenario in a red zone way. Discuss body language, tone and words used. Then ask them to act out the same scenario in a green zone way. Discuss the difference.
2. Introduce phase 1, or the opening phase, of the mediation process – pre-mediation.
3. Introduce the restorative enquiry script. This describes the process of listening to individual accounts of actions, thoughts, feelings and needs in preparation for mediation.
4. The purpose of this is to enable the disputants to both reflect on their responsibilities and to become familiar with the line of questioning mediation uses. It also ascertains whether the people involved are willing to have the mediation meeting.
5. Participation is voluntary, and the process is not able to happen if either party refuses to take part.
6. Discuss:
   The room set-up: The chairs are set in a square fashion to ensure that all participants are treated fairly. The participants sit opposite each other, with the 2 peer mediators sitting opposite each other also.
   Entering the room: It is really important for both participants to be treated the same. Everyone waits outside the room until both participants have arrived. This means all enter together.
   Body language: The role of the peer mediators is to be completely neutral, so their body language needs to be open. Legs and arms are always unfolded, never crossed.
   The mediators' role: The role of the mediators is to maintain a neutral status, never taking sides in any way. This means language, body language and facial expressions must never favour or be seen to support any of the participants (see sheet for ground rules).
7. Ask the CYP to practice setting up the room, welcoming the participants and going through the ground rules with them.
8. Once this has been established, ask them to explore and practice phase 2. Phase 2 involves each of the disputants being asked a set of questions by the mediators. Interruptions are dealt with using a verbal or non-verbal reminder of the ground rules.
9. Phase 3 is then introduced. Phase 3 is focussed on finding the solution to the conflict in ways that are acceptable to both parties, allowing them to move on and repair the rupture in their relationship.
10. Ask the CYP to work in groups and practise the process in the different phases. Ask the groups to watch and give feedback to each other.
11. Finish with a calming relaxation exercise to help the CYP return to the busy classroom or school.

Training part 2: basic skills

GROUND RULES PROMPT

- Welcome

- Can we start by reminding you that you have agreed to be here.

- We/I will not be taking sides.

- We/I will not be judging who is right or wrong.

- Our/my job is to help you sort things out for yourselves.

- We will do this by taking turns to ask questions (like the ones we asked you in our meetings with each of you.)

- We will listen to what you have to say.

- There are two ground rules: First, we will all listen with respect (no butting in, no name calling o put downs.)

- Second, what is said in here stays in here. We will not go out and tell everyone else what has been said. The only expectation is that if we hear something that means you are at risk of harm, we will have to share this with another member of staff.

GROUND RULES PROMPT

Selection and training

RESTORATIVE ENQUIRY SCRIPT

Can you start by telling us what happened?
(Prompt if needed: when? Where? Why?)

What were you thinking at the time?

What were you feeling at the time?

What had happened before between you and ….?

What were your thoughts then?

What were your feelings then?

What has happened since the incident?

What have you been thinking?

What have you been feeling?

Who else has been affected?

Are you willing to have a meeting with …. To sort this out?

Selection and training

RESTORATIVE MEDIATION PROMPT

Mediator 1

Welcome and Ground Rules

Mediator 2 Ask Person 'A':

Can you start by telling us what happened?
(Prompt if needed: when? Where? Why?)

What were you thinking at the time?

What were you feeling at the time?

What had happened before between you and ….?

What were your thoughts then?

What were your feelings then?

What has happened since the incident?

What have you been thinking?

What have you been feeling?

Who else has been affected?

Mediator 2. Ask person B the same questions as Person A

Selection and training

Mediator 1

Ask Person A
What do you need to help sort this out?
Ask Person B
What do you need to help sort this out?

Listen for common ground and summarise, e.g.:
'So you are both saying that you need………..'
'We've heard you both say that ……'

Ask Person A
'What can you do to help move this forward?
Ask Person B
What can you do to help move this forward?

Summarise agreement
'So 'A' you are agreeing to ….'
'So B" you are agreeing to….'

Ask if they want the agreement written down. If yes write the agreement and invite them to sign it.

Make arrangements to follow up and talk to them both about how their agreement and their relationship are going.

Selection and training

Wellbeing Champions training record sheet

Training undertaken:

Date	Name	Signature	Comments

Selection and training

Selection and training

Wellbeing Champions training log sheet

Name:..

As a Wellbeing Champion you will undertake a variety of trainings that will help you deliver support to other children and young people. Please ensure that you fill out your training log sheet after you have undertaken any training and ask the trainer to sign it, saying you have completed the training.

DATE	TRAINING	SIGNATURE	COMMENTS, THOUGHTS AND REFLECTIONS

Selection and training

Selection and training

This Certifies that

....

has successfully completed the training:

....

....

For the role of Wellbeing Champion

Skills include:

Signed:

Selection and training

Wellbeing Champions training feedback

Name: ....

Training: ....
....

Please rate each category on the following scale by placing a tick in the relevant box

1	2	3	4	5
Poor	Satisfactory	Good	Very Good	Excellent

I would very much appreciate your thoughts, experiences, comments and reflections on the training. If there is not enough space on this form, please continue on an additional sheet.

1. Did you enjoy the training?

1	2	3	4	5

Comments:

2. What did you think of the training materials used?

1	2	3	4	5

Comments:

Selection and training

3. What skills did the training focus on?

Comments:

4. What are 3 things you have learnt from the training?

Comments:

5. How do you see yourself practising these skills?

Comments:

6. What was the most interesting thing you learnt from the training?

Comments:

7. In what ways could the training be improved?

Comments:

8. Please write any other comments or reflections.

Selection and training

Calming techniques: my favourite place (P/S)

Time of activity: 25 minutes

Objective

To be able to use a range of techniques to avoid becoming too stressed or overwhelmed by negative emotions

Resources

My Favourite Place sheet

Activity

1. Recap how the body and mind are linked and how the body tries to keep its balance.
2. Ask the children to give examples of the link between the body and mind – e.g. stress and anxiety cause the body to . . .
3. Explain that you are going to teach them another strategy that can calm the body during times of stress or when it feels anxious or overwhelmed.
4. Share the My Favourite Place sheet and ask them to sit quietly and fill it out.
5. Share the different places the children have come up with.
6. Explain to them that the brain is really good at imagining things, so when it imagines their favourite place it makes the body feel as if it is there. This calms the body down and allows it to relax.
7. Ask the children to take some time to sit calmly and think about how their mind and body feel at the moment. Ask them to place how they feel on a calm to stressed spectrum. Then ask them to quietly take themselves in their mind to their favourite place and spend time there for a few minutes. Start at 1 minute and then gradually build up. Set a timer so the children know when to bring their minds back into the room.
8. Explore what it was like for each person. How close did they get to their simile describing their mind and body as being relaxed? Ask the CYP to think of a phrase or way of describing how they feel when they are calm and relaxed. This could be by using a simile. Ask them to share how closely this way of relaxing has enabled them to come to that place of relaxation.
9. Compare this technique with the others you have learnt and ask the children to put them in order of most to least useful/beneficial.
10. Discuss what they have learnt about themselves.
11. Ask if any of them have tried these things for themselves when they have been stressed.

Copyright material from Alison Waterhouse (2021), *Wellbeing Champions*, Routledge

Selection and training

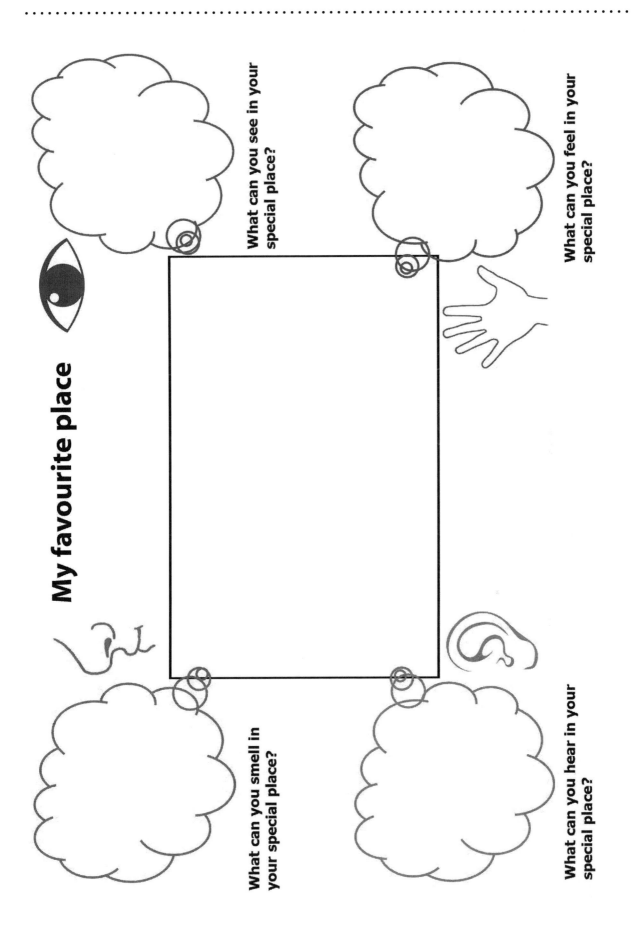

Selection and training

CALMING TECHNIQUES: 5, 4, 3, 2, 1

Calming techniques: 5, 4, 3, 2, 1 (P/S)

Time of activity: 25 minutes

Objective
To be able to use a range of techniques to avoid becoming too stressed or overwhelmed by negative emotions

Resources
5, 4, 3, 2, 1 sheet

Activity

1. Ask the children to think about something that makes them happy. Give them time to feel this and then comment on what you see – smiles, bright eyes, flushed faces, etc. Remind them that by just thinking about something the body responds.
2. Remind the children of the work they have done on stress and of the definition they came up with.
3. Explain that you are going to teach them a strategy that can calm the body during times of stress or when it feels anxious or overwhelmed.
4. Share the 5, 4, 3, 2, 1 sheet and ask them to sit quietly and find the 5, 4, 3, 2, 1 things.
5. Share what the children have found.
6. Explain to them that the brain finds doing two things at a time difficult, so when it is working on the 5, 4, 3, 2, 1 things it is not able to think about other things. This helps calm the mind and this in turn helps calm the body.
7. Explore what it was like for each person. How close did they get to their simile describing their mind and body as being relaxed?
8. Compare this technique with the others you have learnt and ask the children to put them in order of most to least useful/beneficial.
9. Discuss what they have learnt about themselves.
10. Ask if any of them have tried these things for themselves when they have been stressed.

Copyright material from Alison Waterhouse (2021), *Wellbeing Champions*, Routledge

Selection and training

Five Four Three Two One

5 Things you can see

4 Things you can hear

3 Things you can feel

2 Things you can smell

1 Thing you can taste

Selection and training

Calming techniques: visualisation (P/S)

Time of activity: 25 minutes

Objective
To be able to use a range of techniques to avoid becoming too stressed or overwhelmed by negative emotions

Resources
Visualisation sheets

Activity

1. Ask the children to think about a time when they felt happy and relaxed or a time when they felt stressed and unhappy. Explain that you are going to let them think about this for a short while and then, just by looking at them, you are going to say what type of experience they were thinking about.
2. Remind them that the brain and body are linked together and that when the brain is happy the body will feel it. Likewise, if the brain is stressed the body knows something is happening, and it gets ready to fight, flee, flock or freeze.
3. Explain that you are going to teach them a strategy that can calm the body during times of stress or when it feels anxious or overwhelmed.
4. Explain that visualisation is when you take the brain on a journey. It will be a lovely journey and will help them relax their brain and, therefore, their body.
5. Ask the children to sit in a comfortable position and, if they feel able, to close their eyes. Ask them to focus on their breathing and let any thoughts they may have drift away.
6. Start reading the visualisation sheets slowly and with pauses.
7. When you have finished ask the children to take a moment to think about how the experience was for them.
8. Explore what it was like for each person. How close did they get to their simile describing their mind and body as being relaxed?
9. Compare this technique with the others you have learnt and ask the children to put them in order of most to least useful/beneficial.
10. Discuss what they have learnt about themselves.
11. Ask if any of them have tried these things for themselves when they have been stressed.

Calming techniques: visualisation

Selection and training

THE BEACH

Close your eyes and bring yourself to a calm, quiet place in your mind. Just stay here and enjoy the feeling of being relaxed for a little while. Breathe deeply and notice the sound of your breath as it goes in and out. It is a wonderful sound of in and out . . . in and out . . .

(Pause)

Now imagine transporting yourself magically to your favourite place by the sea.

You can choose your favourite place by the sea or imagine a place by the sea you would like to go to.

Picture yourself there now, standing by the sea. You can feel the sand under your feet. It is warm and soft. You are by the sea's edge, and the warm water is gently lapping against your toes. You wiggle your toes in the cool wet sand. It feels good.

The sun is shining brightly and you can feel its warmth on your skin. It feels wonderful. Its warmth soaking into your body makes you feel warm and relaxed. A gentle breeze is blowing off the sea, and it cools you as you stand soaking up the sunshine. It ruffles your hair. You stand still, feeling the sunshine warm you and the gentle breeze blow over you. You feel warm and relaxed.

The smell of the sea fills your nostrils as you breathe in deeply. Overhead you hear the sound of the seagulls calling to each other and the laughter and voices of children splashing in the water. You decide to walk along the beach. You feel the warm water flow over your feet with each wave as it comes. The rhythm of the waves and the water flowing over your feet feel good. They relax you. Your breathing becomes calm and even as you inhale and exhale slowly and calmly like the waves lapping at your feet. Paying attention now, you slow your breathing even further and allow your muscles to relax.

Feel the warmth of the sun melting your muscles into complete relaxation. Slowly and easily your body relaxes more and more . . .

Tension, frustration, worries and doubts all melt away. Inhaling deeply again, breathe in calm and peacefulness.

Your body is now warm and relaxed as you stand on the beach. You are far away in a special place for this moment in time. Your mind is relaxed now too. You can empty your mind of all the tension, worries, thoughts, frustrations and doubts that have been bothering you. You are free to enjoy this moment.

Right now only this matters, relaxing and enjoying this moment. Breathe in deeply and allow the relaxation to flow through your body. Let it flow to the parts that need it. It is warm, calm and peaceful. It spreads through you.

Copyright material from Alison Waterhouse (2021), *Wellbeing Champions*, Routledge

Selection and training

Now let your mind imagine the beautiful, golden, warm sunshine soaking into you, soaking into each and every cell and muscle, flowing through you, making you feel peaceful, calm, relaxed and alive! At this moment in time you can feel the peace that surrounds you, letting you know that everything is all right now.

(Pause)

It is time to return. Take in a deep breath and breathe out. Bring your attention back to where you are . . .

Bring with you the calm, peaceful feelings of relaxation and rest. Now you're feeling energised and peaceful and ready for the rest of your day.

MAGIC CARPET RELAXATION

Take in a deep breath and close your eyes. I'm going to count down from 5 to 1, and when I get to 1 your whole body will feel floppy and heavy and very relaxed. In fact, you will feel so relaxed that you will not even want to move . . . so just stay still and enjoy the wonderful calm feeling that begins to flow into your body.

5 . . . you are starting to feel the calm relaxation flow into your arms and legs.

4 . . . your legs are starting to feel floppy and heavy; your arms start to feel the same too.

3 . . . your whole body now feels calm and relaxed; it feels heavier and heavier and more relaxed and comfortable . . .

2 . . . with every breath you take in and out you feel more and more relaxed.

As I count down the numbers you feel more and more floppy and your body feels like it is floating on air.

As I say 1 . . . your whole body becomes very heavy . . .

Now I want you to imagine that you are lying on a beautiful, colourful carpet. It is a very special carpet. It is a magic carpet. I want you to put out your hand and feel how soft and smooth it is underneath you.

This magic carpet is the most beautiful carpet in the world. It is made of the softest wool and has the most beautiful colours woven into it. The patterns are bright and beautifully woven by very skilled and artistic people.

The people who made the carpet took enormous care with it. They loved making the carpet, and you can feel that love and care around you gently holding you. They made this very special magical carpet just for you. There is no other in the whole world quite like this. It is unique and very special.

I want you to put out your hands and find the special tassels that hang down from each of the front corners of the carpet. As you touch them the tassels become hard and strong and stick straight up like handles . . . you feel perfectly safe.

The magic carpet gently moves. It is getting ready to take you on a very special journey. You feel safe and curious about where you will go and what you will see. Gently it moves, slowly at first. It doesn't want to frighten you. You feel safe and comfortable. You know the magic carpet is strong and will look after you, but you are also keen to start your adventure. The magic carpet gently sways and flies up. It makes you giggle with delight and excitement! What an adventure! It takes you up into the sky, higher and higher, up to the soft, fluffy white clouds that surround you like the softest of cotton wool. It's wonderful to be here . . . feeling free and completely relaxed. You can breathe clearly here. You inhale deeply and exhale slowly. You love the feel of floating in the clouds. Your body feels light and full of calm. You gently float along, watching the white clouds gently bump and play around you. They make you smile. You look down and see the beautiful green patches below you. The fields and hedges are tiny and stretch out below like a big green carpet. The trees seem to wave at you whilst the wind gently blows their branches back and forth. You can see fields and woods, ponds and rivers, mountains and hills all passing slowly below you. As you watch you see houses that look quite tiny from all the way up here.

As you float gently along all your worries seem to leave you, soaking into the clouds all around you, soaked up like blotting paper. All problems and difficult thoughts you had seem to disappear, and your mind feels calm and relaxed and as if it has a big smile inside. As you are gently blown along by the breeze, all your worries and problems are left far, far behind you. This is a beautiful carpet ride. You are now ready for the carpet to play. First it swoops and turns . . . then it twirls and flies up and down. You can feel laughter growing inside you as you swirl and turn up and down like you're on your very own magical roller coaster. You love the feeling of the wind in your hair and the clouds gently touching your hands. You laugh again, and the laughter makes the clouds wobble as if they are laughing too. You can go as fast as you want or as slow as you would like. You play, one minute going fast and the next going slow. You are in full control. Up, down and around you steer. Faster and faster, higher and higher, then down and down. Slower, faster – you choose . . .

What an amazing ride up in the sky.

Now it is time to slow down and gradually stop. Take in a deep breath and glide your magic carpet back down to the ground. Gently, it lands on the ground and comes to a stop when you're ready. As you land think of all the wonderful, happy feelings you have and bring them back with you. When you are ready open your eyes. Breathe in deeply and breathe out. Do this a couple of times. You've done a fantastic job of using your imagination!

Selection and training

RELAXATION: FLYING HIGH LIKE A BUTTERFLY

Close your eyes and take in a nice deep breath. Breathe in through your nose and out through your mouth. Breathe in again and feel the wonderful air flow into your lungs.

Allow your tummy to fill up like a balloon and then exhale slowly. Do this 5 times to really relax your whole body completely.

(Pause for breathing)

Your body begins to feel deeply relaxed, and you can feel it grow heavy as the calmness flows through your arms, legs and body. It feels good, like warm sunshine flowing through you. Your legs begin to feel very heavy. Your arms begin to feel heavy and relaxed. You enjoy every moment as your body continues to relax with each word I say.

As your body relaxes, imagine you're a beautiful butterfly, gently standing on a flower in a wonderful garden. Around you, you can hear the gentle humming of bees and the breeze gently flowing through the branches of the tress. The sunshine is filling the garden with warmth and yellow light. Around you birds are singing and you can hear a lawn mower in the distance cutting the grass. You watch as a small brown bird flies above you. You remember you have beautiful wings folded up and decide that you would like to fly in the breeze and see the garden from above. You flap your wings and gracefully rise into the air, fluttering up into the sky.

As you look down you can see the green fields and hedges below you like a huge patchwork quilt. You can see the lovely green valley below you with lots of colourful flowers, just waiting for you to enjoy.

You feel the wind blow against your delicate wings.

As the wind touches your beautiful wings, it gently blows away any worries and any stress you feel. You feel your worries and stress blow off into the sky. It feels wonderful to be free of them. Your mind is clear and calm. It feels as though it is full of sunshine and smiles. The worries are now left far behind you. You feel relaxed and happy as you gracefully fly in the sky. Happiness flows through your body, making your wings strong and beautiful.

The sun gently touches your body and warms you. Big, white, fluffy clouds float above you in the blue sky, gently bumping into each other and playing hide and seek. Their silliness and happiness make you giggle. You are warm and relaxed as you fly in the breeze, watching the green fields and trees below you. A ribbon of silver twists across the green below as you notice a river sparkling in the sunlight. It looks wonderful. You are enjoying each moment here in the sky, gliding along, feeling calm and peaceful. You spread your wings far and stretch.

It feels so good. Your body is calm and your mind is peaceful.

Selection and training

Calming techniques: soles of my feet (P/S)

Time of activity: 25 minutes

Objective

To be able to use a range of techniques to avoid becoming too stressed or overwhelmed by negative emotions

Resources

Meditation on the soles of my feet

Activity

1. Ask the children and young people to think of a time when they were calm, relaxed and at ease.
2. Ask them to share these moments with each other.
3. Ask them to explore how their mind and body felt. If it was a colour, what would it be? Would it be the same for both mind and body?
4. Create a simile to describe it: My mind was calm and relaxed like a . . . My body felt like . . . .
5. Now ask them about a time when they were overwhelmed with a negative emotion. Ask them to share the emotion and the situation.
6. Pose the question, How useful would it be if you had a range of strategies to help you manage when you became overwhelmed?
7. Explain that different people enjoy using different strategies, so you have to learn and play with a range before you can choose the one that works best for you.
8. One of these strategies is meditation on the soles of your feet. Ask the children to sit in a comfortable position and go through the meditation.
9. Explore what it was like for each person. How close did they get to their simile describing their mind and body as being relaxed?

Copyright material from Alison Waterhouse (2021), *Wellbeing Champions*, Routledge

Selection and training

SOLES OF MY FEET

If you are standing, stand in a natural, relaxed posture with your arms hanging by your sides and your knees slightly bent and with the soles of your feet flat on the floor. If you are sitting, sit comfortably with the soles of your feet flat on the floor.

1. Breathe naturally and do nothing.

2. Now shift all your attention to the soles of your feet.

3. Slowly move your toes.

4. Feel your shoes covering your feet. Feel the texture of your socks or tights.

5. Notice the temperature of your feet. Are they warm or cool?

6. How light or heavy do they feel?

7. Now notice the connection with the surface beneath your feet.

8. Take a moment and focus on how your feet feel.

9. Feel the heels of your feet against the back of your shoes. If you do not have shoes on, feel the floor or carpet with the soles of your feet.

10. Wiggle your toes and think about how they feel next to each other.

11. Do your feet tingle? Feel heavy or light? Notice how they feel.

12. Allow your mind to just focus on your feet for a while.

13. Slow down your breathing a little and imagine your blood picking up oxygen in your lungs and taking it down to your feet. The blood flows down your leg, into your foot. It flows around your foot, along each of your toes, bringing new oxygen and energy to them.

14. Continue breathing in deeply and let the blood carry the oxygen into your feet. Do this three times.

15. Now gradually let yourself see the room you are in. Think about your whole body. When you are ready, give your hands a shake and then notice how you feel in comparison to how you felt when you started.

Copyright material from Alison Waterhouse (2021), *Wellbeing Champions*, Routledge

Selection and training

Friendship bench 	Body language Active listening Recognising and understanding emotions Resolving conflict Playground games
Drop in lunchtime group 	Body language Active listening Recognising and understanding emotions Resolving conflict Problem solving Self-image/Self-awareness
Peer mediators 	Body language Active listening Recognising and understanding emotions Resolving conflict Points of view Problem solving
WBC notice board 	Core training
Transition support 	Body language Active listening Recognising and understanding emotions

Selection and training

Assemblies	Core training
Promote a healthy lifestyle – special events programme	Core training Self-image/Self-awareness
Playground buddies	Body language Active listening Recognising and understanding emotions Resolving conflict Problem solving
Student listeners	Body language Active listening Recognising and understanding emotions Resolving conflict Problem solving
Revision buddies	Active listening Recognising and understanding emotions Problem solving Revision strategies

Chapter 3

Supervision: Reflective practice

Supervision

REFLECTIVE PRACTICE

Reflective practice is a way of studying our own experiences and, in so doing, improving and developing our thinking and the way we work with others. Reflective practice is extremely useful in helping us understand and learn how to extend our ability to learn in the future.

The act of reflection is a powerful way to increase our understanding of what is both known and not known. It is a way to develop confidence in our own abilities as a learner, and it enables us to be curious and to return to and think about a situation and understand it more fully. It enables us to think about the part we played in it and how other people experienced our interactions. The benefits of reflective practice include:

- increased learning from an experience or situation
- promotion of greater understanding or deeper learning
- identification of personal strengths and areas that may benefit us if developed
- identification of skills or knowledge that may benefit us if developed
- acquisition of new knowledge and skills

REFLECTIVE PRACTICE WITHIN A GROUP

Developing a group reflective practice is a way of helping all individuals within the group share an experience and then reflect on their understanding of that experience, including their subsequent actions. This reflection on thoughts, feelings and actions enables our experiences and actions to be more fully explored and understood. The art of being curious about what we have experienced and how we have felt and thought about this is often leads to greater self-awareness and understanding.

When developing group reflective practices it is essential to ensure that the group understand both the purpose and the role the group provides for the individual. For an individual to share their thoughts and understanding of a situation, they need to feel safe and respected. For the group, it is important to explore and fully understand what this actually means and how they can ensure that their actions, language and behaviours reflect this.

WHAT IS SUPERVISION?

Supervision is about creating a space and a relationship where sharing, reflecting and supporting enable another person to make progress, develop skills or feel "able" in a particular area or with a piece of work they are undertaking. A supervisory relationship is one in which a person with some knowledge and skill takes responsibility and accountability for the wellbeing and performance of the person being supervised – the supervisee. This is about developing a supportive, rather than judgemental, thinking space in which to reflect and understand thoughts, feelings, actions or the work being undertaken. If supervision is to be successful it is essential for the supervisor to develop a positive and safe relationship with the supervisee and to ensure that they have the time and space to develop this support. Good supervision enables people to:

- build effective and trusted relationships

- develop positive skills and ways of working

- exercise good judgement and make valuable decisions

- improve the quality of whatever they are working on

Ineffective supervision can damage the relationship or culture within the environment in which it is based.

REFLECTIVE GROUP SUPERVISION

Reflective group supervision takes from both reflective practice and supervision models to create a safe, trusted and informed space for the Wellbeing Champions to share, think and explore the work they have been undertaking. The importance of the supervision aspect is to ensure the safety and wellbeing of the Champions themselves. This aspect of the work will come from the WBC Facilitator, who will lead and facilitate the reflective group supervision.

WHY IS IT IMPORTANT?

By setting up reflective group supervision sessions the CYP can share and discuss the work they have been doing. This ensures a shared sense of work and enables a greater understanding of different aspects of the work they may be involved in. It is like constant teaching, as every piece of work they share and reflect on allows others in the group to learn and develop skills, knowledge and understanding. Four key aspects of reflective group supervision are:

1. Ensuring that the CYP they are supporting are safe and that any difficulties are quickly picked up and dealt with by trained staff or referred on to specialist support. It is really vital to remember that the WBC role is not to support CYP with a high level of need; it is a phase 1 support system.

2. Ensuring that the WBC are looked after and supported in their role within the school.

Supervision

3. Supporting their understanding that they can help in a variety of ways, one of which is by providing direct support and another is by ensuring that trained staff are brought in when needed.

4. Ensuring that the work being undertaken is thought about, reflected on and safe and is reflective of the ethos of the school and its community.

DIFFERENT WAYS SUPERVISION CAN BE UNDERTAKEN

Supervision with the WBC can be undertaken in a variety of ways. However, it is important to ensure that it is regular and weekly and facilitated by the Wellbeing Champions Facilitator. The number of WBC will dictate whether there is one group or two. This therefore needs consideration at the beginning of the project. Groups work best when they have between 6 and 10 members. This enables time for each person to talk and share the work they have been doing and also allows time for conversations and teaching moments around this. If the group is too large and you are working with another member of staff, I would suggest that you divide the Champions into two smaller groups so that you can supervise one group each. It is really important to remember that if one of you is not able to take your group, the other member of staff will need to step in. When supervision gets forgotten or postponed, the WBC struggle and people either forget to pass on information or information is overlooked. This can be dangerous.

Groups can be supervised whenever it is most suitable for your school environment. One of the nicest supervision groups I ever worked with met over lunchtime, with all bringing a packed lunch and sharing what we had. This community lunch became a real focal point, and at times we all made something special for the group to share. Cakes and biscuits were always popular – even my courgette cake!

Groups can also be supervised during the day or after school – whichever is most suitable for your environment. The golden rule is that supervision occurs each week at the same time and is undertaken by the same person. This regularity ensures that the CYP know they have a space where they are supported and listened to. Often just knowing this is enough to contain their feelings, worries and questions.

CONFIDENTIALITY AND SUPERVISION

Helping the WBC understand how to use the reflective space is a really interesting journey. In the beginning many will share the factual aspect of their work but few will extend this and share how they felt or how they acted and their thinking behind this. As the group develops and they understand the non-judgemental way of working, they will gradually start to share their thoughts and understandings of what has been going on and will start to question and be curious about the differences we all have in understanding and interpreting situations and interactions.

It is useful to start the work by sharing a piece of work you have undertaken with a student and your thoughts, emotions and understanding – reflections of what happened and why. This allows the WBC to experience the process as well as the way you ensure that the person's identity can stay confidential if needed. It is always best to try and ensure this within the group supervision situation. Explain the background and why you stepped in or were approached and how that made you feel. Share the conversation and any clues you picked up during this phase. Then share the technique you may have used – active listening, reflection of their statements to allow them to expand on them, co-regulation techniques or language. Share how the situation developed and how you have thought about it since. Ask for any questions or suggestions about what you did and why and then share what you have done as a follow-up.

It is important for the WBC to understand that within group supervision it is useful to try not to name people but to focus on the interaction or event. However, in their follow-up notes – which are a record of the work they do and which the group facilitator sees – they can use initials. If during supervision you feel that a piece of work a Wellbeing Champion has been involved in needs a longer discussion, or they have struggled with it in any way, you may ask them to meet you in a 1:1 supervision session. This 1:1 session enables you to discuss the work/interaction more fully. During this time it would be important to know the other young person involved, so their name can now be shared. It is important for you to keep a record of any 1:1 supervision session you ask for and to ensure that any information is carefully recorded. Confidentiality and how to handle this within sessions and supervision are a core part of the training. It is really important to gently remind young people both why confidentiality is important and how the system works. Reminding the Champions that at no time can they promise not to share information is also an important point that enables you as the facilitator to keep all safe and supported.

RECORDING SUPERVISION

Recording supervision sessions is really important. Within the reflective group supervision the WBC can take turns in recording the discussion. The record sheet (see example) needs to reflect who attended, any apologies, what each WBC shared with the group, any decisions that came out of this and any follow-up that needed to happen. It can also record any training that might be needed as a follow-up to the work they have been involved in. An example of this might be that the new Friendship Bench on the playground has been used several times by children who have fallen out with their friends. The Friendship Mentors have struggled with knowing or being able to support the repair of these friendships, so training them in restorative practices would be a way of supporting a new need that has been identified.

Supervision

All supervision notes need to be kept in a safe and secure location. You may find that information needs to be passed on to other members of staff or added to school recording systems. If this is the case, ensure that this is also recorded on your supervision record.

REFERRAL PATHWAYS

When you set up support systems within any organisation you will find situations where the help that is needed is far greater than you can offer safely. It matters not on which level you work. There are always situations that arise that need more. What is really important is that you know the pathways available to you and what member of staff is leading each one. As with any safeguarding situation, it is far better to pass on information and share your concerns or thoughts than not. If in doubt, talk to the member of staff who leads that area and share your concerns.

Within your school there will be staff who lead teaching and learning, heads of years or pastoral support staff, wellbeing leads or safeguarding leads, all of whom have immense knowledge, training and experience. They are there to help, support and enable you to make the decision about which way to go.

Along with referring to another specialised member of staff may be a wish to find out more about a particular issue. There are many charities and support groups that specialise in particular areas that you can access online and that will add to your own knowledge, understanding and ability to think about, support and help others. It is important, however, that you recognise that you are a practitioner who wishes to support others within a school setting. You are not a specialised mental health practitioner.

SUPERVISION OF THE PROJECT FACILITATOR

You have now set up your reflective group supervision space for the WBC and have a range of good systems in place to support or work with the different needs you have come across. But what about you? The wellbeing of your WBC depends on you. You are their role model, so you have to model how you look after yourself. Why should they come to supervision once a week if you don't set up your own? Why should they reflect on how they speak to and work and interact with people if you don't do the same? If you are working with another member of staff, you can set up your own reflective space where you can talk and think together about the work you are involved in. If you are working and leading the project on your own, then you will need to set up a supervision or reflective space of your own. Whichever route you choose, it is really important that you put something in place for yourself and any other staff involved in the project.

Supervision

TEACHING WBC TO LOOK AFTER THEMSELVES

When you are drawn into the field of supporting or caring for others it is really important that you ensure that you look after and care for yourself. If you do not, your wellbeing will ultimately suffer. This often means that the support you have put in place is not robust enough and thus collapses.

Many of the WBC will continue to work in the way they have now been trained. They are often the ones who go on to the caring professions, so it is important that you build in and teach ways they can use to look after themselves whilst looking after others. Help them to understand that it is not being selfish to look after their own wellbeing and that by doing this they model this way of being for others and ensure that the support they give can continue.

So what ways can you teach or help them to develop? I have tried to build into the training a variety of ways, such as visualisation, breathing techniques, mindfulness and reflective spaces. You can also support their development by teaching them how to be their own best friend, helping them gain an understanding of the importance of nature and discussing healthy ways to take time out and relax, such as listening to music, reading or watching films. Being interested in what they do to relax is often enough to send the message that relaxation is not only important but also vital.

Celebration of the work and the group is also important. In addition, finding the opportunity to say "thank you" and "well done" whilst also enabling them to be together as a group is important and can be easily built into the school timetable. When running groups I always tried to do something each term that was fun and relaxing – Easter egg hunts, Christmas scavenger hunts, secret Santas, birthday cake and cards, summer picnics – as a way to say "thank you."

SUMMARY REPORTS FOR THE SENIOR LEADERSHIP TEAM

At the end of each term it is beneficial to write a WBC Summary Report for the Senior Leadership Team. The team is then able to explore the work and support new developments or training needs that have arisen. Within secondary schools it is useful if children and young people can share in this report, collecting information during the term and adding feedback from CYP who have used their support, or from the WBC themselves. Ensuring the CYP are involved enables them to learn new skills and evaluate the project at regular intervals.

Within the report it is useful to highlight the work the WBC are undertaking and how this may have changed due to needs now identified, the number of children using the support, referrals made, the reasons for these referrals, feedback from both the WBC and those they support and any safeguarding issues that have arisen, including how these were dealt with and by whom.

SPECIFIC ISSUES THAT MAY ARISE

When any new project starts a range of difficult issues are likely to emerge. How you help both the Champions and others think about and consider these is important to the way the project will develop. Take each one as an opportunity to grow and develop the best possible provision you can. Ensure that the issues are shared with the CYP (if appropriate) so that you can use the opportunity to support their problem-solving skills and help them think about the whole school and not just the WBC part.

Record the journey so that you can help other people understand how the project has developed or share with other schools. Recording can be undertaken in many different ways, but photos and direct feedback are often the most useful. One really good way to share the work and ensure that people understand what you do and how is to create a Wellbeing Champions movable display that is full of CYP working in different areas, quotes from the CYP who have used the support and useful addresses or information. The display can then be brought out each time the school opens its doors to parents or visitors and the WBC can share the work they have been doing and talk to interested adults and other young people. This allows mental health and wellbeing to be openly talked about, demonstrates what your school is doing and how and provides a forum for people to find out more information about different areas.

REVIEW AND DEVELOP PRACTICE

At the end of each term it is really worthwhile to gather all the WBC together and review the work they have been involved in. Get them used to expressing their ideas and opinions and also backing these up with evidence. An example of this might be, "I think the WBC Friendship Bench has proved a great idea, and lots of children have used it." This is a personal opinion. However, if they can then back this up with evidence it becomes much more powerful. An example of this might be, "The Friendship Bench in the infants' playground has been used by over 50 children this term. The reasons the children have given for liking this are the following: It has helped me make friends with children in year 2 (child in year R). It has helped me know what to do when I argue with my friends (child in year 2). It has helped me to like playtime now, as I know there are always people to play with (child in year 1)." This then allows the children to take this evidence and think about how to develop the work they are doing in the future. It might lead to the children suggesting an extension of the idea, Would a Friendship Bench in the junior playground be helpful? Supporting the children in asking the question and then thinking about how to find the answer is a great learning opportunity. This review helps the children create the report for the SLT on their work and uncover why they might wish to develop certain areas.

Supervision

RESOURCES

Reflective Group Supervision Record Sheet
Individual Supervision Record Sheet
Wellbeing Champions Reflective Group Supervision Record Sheet
Referral Forms
Summary Sheet for Senior Leadership Team on the Work of the WBC for the Term

Supervision

REFLECTIVE GROUP SUPERVISION RECORD SHEET	
Date:	Supervisor:
Wellbeing Champions present:	
Apologies:	
Feedback from individuals:	
Feedback continued:	
Follow-up actions (What these are and who will do them)	

Supervision

Safeguarding issues raised:
Training issues highlighted:
Signature of supervisor:

Copyright material from Alison Waterhouse (2021), *Wellbeing Champions*, Routledge

Supervision

INDIVIDUAL SUPERVISION RECORD SHEET	
Date:	Supervisor:

Wellbeing Champion:

Reason for individual supervision:

Discussion:

Follow-up actions (what these will be and who will do them)

Supervision

Safeguarding issues raised:

Training issues highlighted:

Signature of supervisor:

Signature of Wellbeing Champion:

Supervision

WELLBEING CHAMPIONS REFLECTIVE GROUP SUPERVISION RECORD SHEET

Supervision undertaken by:

....

DATE	NAME	SIGNATURE	COMMENTS

Supervision

Supervision

WELLBEING CHAMPIONS REFERRAL RECORD SHEET

Date:	Supervisor:

Referral to:

Reason for referral:

Information to support referral:

Supervision

Safeguarding issues:

Any other comments:

Signature of supervisor:

Feedback from referral process:	Date of feedback:

Supervision

SUMMARY OF WBC WORK FOR SENIOR LEADERSHIP TEAM

Term:

Date:	WBC Facilitator:

Support in place and how this has been used this term (including numbers):

Feedback from individuals being supported:

Supervision

Feedback from WBC offering support:
Safeguarding issues raised:
Referrals made (to which area, including numbers):
Areas covered in supervision:

Supervision

Training issues highlighted:

Any other issues highlighted:

Actions required:

Signature of Wellbeing Champions Facilitator:

Supervision

Feedback from SLT:

Actions required (by whom and when):

Head teacher's signature:

Date:

Chapter 4
Learn, talk and share: Developing the role of the Wellbeing Champions

Learn, talk and share

REVIEW, CHECK AND SHARE

At the end of each stage it is really good to review what you have done with the CYP and to think about what they have enjoyed, what they have found useful and what they have taken away.

Whilst working you have collected a variety of feedback information, including information on the interview process, the training and the work as the Wellbeing Champions have been doing it. You have also been collecting information from the CYP who have used the different supports or interventions you have introduced. It is a useful exercise to share these with the CYP and to record them on a termly evaluation sheet that can then be discussed by you and the CYP with the SLT at the end of each term. This process will enable you to plan the following term. Support you plan the following term. If only 2 CYP have used the lunchtime drop-in, then it may be better to cut back on the sessions or to focus your time and energy on another area. If this is the case, make sure you talk to the 2 children who have used the drop-in and support them in finding something else they can do, as they may rely on this activity.

This review can also highlight a need, such as that children using the Friendship Bench are often trying to manage arguments or falling out. This could lead to a set of sessions in class looking at friendships and what to do when they go wrong or an assembly on supporting others. It may highlight the need for additional training. For instance, if conflict has been identified as an area that needs support, the WBC may need conflict resolution training to help the children and young people on the playground.

At each stage, help the children understand the importance of collecting information and then sitting down and analysing what they have collected. This will help them understand the importance of collecting information and asking in-depth questions about the results they may have gathered as well as the process of developing the project and sharing what they have been doing and how it has supported other CYP.

UPDATE TRAINING

As you start work it will become clear as to whether the CYP have the skills to meet the needs you have identified or if their training needs to be adapted, added to or changed in any way.

Thoughts about this are reflected on the group reflective supervision notes each week and so can be easily accessed and then discussed with the WBC at the end of the term. The children can be encouraged to request training they think might be useful. In one school in which I worked, all the children requested first aid as a way of helping on the playground and in their lives outside school.

As the CYP work with others it will be clear if they have the skills needed to continue with the different projects or if their skills need to be extended. If the CYP supporting the drop-in feel they have a lot of autistic CYP who use the facility, they may ask to have some training in this field. If the work supporting children transitioning into the school from another school identifies the need for a "welcome to our school" user pack for CYP, the Wellbeing Champions might lead a session within classes to put together a pack created by other CYP.

Another area to think about is your own training needs. Have there been areas you wished you knew more about? Would it be good to extend your skills and knowledge? Your skills, knowledge and understanding are also really important, so make sure these are included in your thinking and planning.

RECRUITING THE NEXT COHORT

As the year goes on, some children will move or transition out of the school and your WBC will decrease in number, so you will need to think about how and when to run the recruitment again to replenish your numbers. It is so much easier the second time, as you now have the first lot of WBC to help you. Take the opportunity of recruitment to ensure that they are fully involved and talk to them about how to run the recruitment and the interviews – maybe they can interview the candidates along with yourself as the facilitator.

How you will involve the WBC in the training is another really important area to think about, plan and implement. I have always found it really useful to have a few established WBC in the training, as they can share their experiences of working with others and undergoing the training and supervision. Each cohort tends to take on a special group feeling – with some crossover – but I think the fact that they experience the process and training as a group brings them closer together.

You need to remember that, having done the recruitment and training once already, you have also learnt a lot, so you bring that new knowledge and experience to the next group.

Having already got an established group of WBC means that you now have the added benefit of pairing new and old together, and I have always found that setting up a buddy system is a great way to help both the new and the trained understand the work and extend their knowledge and expertise. It also means that you are not always the first point of call for a question, and that can really help.

TALK, LEARN AND SHARE

Now that you have reviewed and identified the things that have gone well, not so well or really need to change and have trained enough CYP for the year ahead, it is worth thinking about how you can start to meet up with other schools with similar schemes in place and talk, share and learn new ways or practices. This can be a really exciting and rich experience for you and the CYP. One way of doing this is to nominate 2–4 Wellbeing Champions as ambassadors. If there are other

Learn, talk and share

schools in your local area you could organise a meeting for the ambassadors once a term and take turns hosting a morning and bringing them all together for a specific event, discussion or training. This will allow good practice to be shared and will enable you to meet likeminded people who have chosen a similar journey.

This could be turned into an annual event, with a yearly WBC conference at which each school can present an aspect of their work; speakers can be invited to share their experiences and new schools can see the work you are all involved in.

 **RESOURCES**

Termly Evaluation Sheet

Learn, talk and share

SUMMARY OF WBC WORK FOR SENIOR LEADERSHIP TEAM

Term:	
Date:	WBC Facilitator:
Support in place and how this has been used this term (including numbers):	
Feedback from individuals being supported:	
Feedback from WBC offering support:	

Learn, talk and share

Safeguarding issues raised:

Referrals made (to which area, including numbers):

Areas covered in supervision:

Learn, talk and share

Training issues highlighted:

Any other issues highlighted:

Actions required:

Learn, talk and share

Signature of Wellbeing Champions Facilitator:
Feedback from SLT:
Actions required (by whom and when):
Head teacher's signature:
Date:

References

Baginsky, W. (2004). Peer mediation in the UK: A guide for schools. *NSPCC Inform*. Retrieved from www.nspcc.org.uk/inform/resourcesforteachers/classroomresources/peermediationintheuk_wda48928.html

Cowie, H., & Smith, P. K. (2010). Peer support as a means of improving school safety and reducing bullying and violence. In B. Doll, W. Pfohl, & J. Yoon (Eds.), *Handbook of youth prevention science* (pp. 177–193). New York: Routledge.

Cowie, H., & Wallace, P. (2000). *Peer support in action*. London: Sage.

Department for Children, Schools and Families. (2007/0212). Ed Balls announces £3m for anti-bullying pilots. *Press Notice*. Retrieved from www.dcsf.gov.uk/pns/DisplayPN.cgi?pn_id=2007_0212

Department for Children, Schools and Families. (2008). *Formalised peer mentoring pilot evaluation*. DCSF-RR033.

Department for Education. (2017). *Peer support and children and young people's mental health*. Research Review. Nick Coleman, Wendy Sykes and Carola Groom, Independent Social Research (ISR).

Dodge, R., Daly, A. P., Huyton, J., & Sanders, L. D. (2012). The challenge of defining wellbeing. *International Journal of Wellbeing, 2*(3).

Ford, T., Parker, C., Salim, J., Goodman, R., Logan, S., & Henley, W. (2018). The relationship between exclusion from school and mental health: A secondary analysis of the British Child and Adolescent Mental Health Surveys 2004 and 2007. *Psychological Medicine, 48*(4), 629–641.

Government Statistical Service. (2017). *Mental health of children and young people in England*. Retrieved from https://digital.nhs.uk/data-and-information/publications/statistical/mental-health-of-children-and-young-people-in-england/2017/2017

Houlston, C., Smith, P. K., & Jessel, J. (2009). Investigating the extent and use of peer support initiatives in English schools. *Educational Psychology, 29*, 325–344.

References

Kessler, R. C., Berglund, P., Demler, O., Jin, R., Merikangas, K. R., & Walters, E. E. (2005). Lifetime prevalence and age-of-onset distributions of DSM-IV disorders in the National Comorbidity Survey replication. *Archives of General Psychiatry, 62*(6), 593–602. https://doi.org/10.1001/archpsyc.62.6.593.

MBF. (2011). *Department of Education Peer support and children and young people's mental health*. Research Review 2017. Retrieved from https://assets.publishing.service.gov.uk/government/uploads/system/uploads/attachment_data/file/603107/Children_and_young_people_s_mental_health_peer_support.pdf

Murphey, D., Barry, M., & Vaughn, B. (2013). Positive mental health: Resilience. *Adolescent Health Highlight, 3,* 1–6.

Naylor, P., & Cowie, H. (1999). The effectiveness of peer support systems in challenging school bullying: The perspectives and experiences of teachers and pupils. *Journal of Adolescence, 22,* 467–479.

Public Health England. (2019). *The mental health and wellbeing joint strategic needs assessment*. Retrieved from www.gov.uk/government/publications/better-mental-health-jsna-toolkit/5-children-and-young-people

Salmivalli, C. (1999). Participant role approach to school bullying: Implications for interventions. *Journal of Adolescence, 22,* 453–459.

Salmivalli, C. (2001). Peer-led intervention campaign against school bullying: Who considered it useful, who benefited? *Educational Research, 43*(3), 263–278.

Smith, P. K., & Samara, M. (2003). *Evaluation of the DfES anti-bullying pack*. Research Brief No. RBX06-03. DfES, London.

Toda, Y. (2005). Bullying and peer support systems in Japan. In D. W. Shwalb, J. Nakazawa, & B. J. Shwalb (Eds.), *Applied developmental psychology: Theory, practice, and research from Japan* (pp. 301–319). Greenwich, CT: Information Age Publishing Inc.

United Nations. (1991). *United Nations convention on the rights of the child*. Innocenti. Studies. Florence: UNICEF.

WHO. (2003). *Caring for children and adolescents with mental disorders: Setting WHO directions* [online]. Geneva: World Health Organization.

World Health Organisation. (2014). *Mental health: A state of wellbeing*. Retrieved from http://origin.who.int/features/factfiles/mental_health/en/